SHOP STEWARDS AND SHOP COMMITTEES

Towards Industrial Peace in Australia (1937)

Solving Labour Problems in Australia (1941)

Wartime Labour Developments in Australia (1943)

Industrial Regulation in Australia (1947)

Studies in Australian Labour Law and Relations (1952)

Better Employment Relations and Other Essays in Labour (1954)

Developments in the Law Governing Workers Compensation in Victoria (1956)

Industrial Conciliation and Arbitration in Australia (1959)

Trade Unionism in Australia (1962)

SHOP STEWARDS AND SHOP COMMITTEES

*A Study in Trade Unionism and
Industrial Relations in Australia*

ORWELL de R. FOENANDER

*formerly Associate Professor in Industrial Relations
University of Melbourne*

MELBOURNE UNIVERSITY PRESS

LONDON AND NEW YORK: CAMBRIDGE UNIVERSITY PRESS

First published 1965
Printed and bound in Australia by
Melbourne University Press, Carlton N.3, Victoria
Registered in Australia for transmission
by post as a book

Text set in 11 point Fairfield type

PREFACE

The author had in mind the inclusion of chapters dealing with workers shop stewards, and shop stewards committees, in a study on trade unionism in which he was engaged some little time back. He concluded, however, that their insertion would not conform with the particular design and general plan ultimately adopted for the work and that, in any case, the matters to be covered by these chapters were of such consequence and of so interesting a character as to merit consideration in a volume reserved to themselves. Accordingly these matters were deferred for a later treatment, and the present publication embodying some of the results of the treatment may be regarded in a sense —but only in a sense—as an adjunct to the book in question which has already made its appearance.

The lack of attention to these matters on the part of writers on trade unionism and labour relations in the Australian setting is surprising, seeing that shop stewards (or their equivalent under another name) and shop committees have been operative in Australian industrial establishments, and on the jobs, over a considerable number of years. The position in this respect is in sharp contrast with that of other countries of importance, for example, the United States and Great Britain, where the part played by these persons and bodies in the factories and the various outside employments has attracted increasingly critical investigation by writers on industrial subjects. The function and activities of shop stewards and their committees, moreover, are not without their significance in the social and political, as well as the industrial, life of the country. It is hoped that this publication will provide some modest compensation in reparation for past neglects.

CONTENTS

ABBREVIATIONS

A.C.	Appeal Cases (decisions of the House of Lords and Privy Council)
Act	Conciliation and Arbitration Act 1904-1964, unless the context indicates otherwise
A.R. (N.S.W.)	Arbitration Reports (New South Wales)
C.A.R.	Commonwealth Arbitration Reports
Ch.	Chancery (decisions of the Chancery Division of the High Court of Justice)
C.L.R.	Commonwealth Law Reports
Commission	Commonwealth Conciliation and Arbitration Commission, unless the context indicates otherwise
Court	Commonwealth Industrial Court, unless the context indicates otherwise
F.L.R.	Federal Law Reports
K.B.	King's Bench (decisions of the King's Bench Division of the High Court of Justice)

1

INTRODUCTION

Communist Interest in Shop Stewards and Committees

In Australia in recent years workers shop stewards and shop stewards committees, both institutionally and as operating persons or bodies, have come to command increasing attention in industrial and other quarters. Integrally, however, they remain of lesser importance in the edifice of its trade unionism and, all things considered, they continue to play a subordinate and comparatively minor part in the general conduct of labour relations in this country. But that is not to say that there have been of late no movements of significance in relation to them, and the changes that have, in fact, occurred must be assessed as in some respects strengthening, while in other respects weakening, the machinery of Australian trade unionism and the facilities for its normal application.[1] A measure of the increase in this attention is, without doubt, assignable to the close—and even intense—interest that has been manifested by Communist and other left-wing connections in the potentialities of the shop committees, and to the endeavours of Communist factors to enlist a decisive influence in the behaviour of these bodies.

To Communists throughout the world the trade union is, as taught by Nikolai Lenin, one of the chief media for the propagation of their ideologies and the ensuring of success for plans to give effect to their theories.[2] In order to gain a footing in a

---

[1] With respect to the case of Great Britain, V. L. Allen, *Power in Trade Unions* (London, 1954), p. 184, says: 'Shop stewards and branch officials, in so far as they are in direct contact with the rank and file and frequently determine the temper of the ordinary workers, carry a heavy responsibility in industrial relations; because they are primarily responsible for recruitment and for communicating executive decisions to the rank and file members they hold positions of responsibility within the organizations too.' For the importance attached to the shop steward in the United States see Jack Barbash, *Labor's Grass Roots* (New York, 1961), p. 112.

[2] 'It is impossible to win over the vast proletarian masses unless the trade

union with orthodox views and divert its intentions to the pursuit of Communist ends, the Communist Party in Australia (as it is called) tries to fill with its own candidates as many offices and other superior posts in the union hierarchy or structure as possible, especially the general and branch presidencies and vicepresidencies, general and branch secretaryships, and organizerships, as well as memberships of the central committee of management and the branch or district committees of management.[3] When disappointed at the ballots in the quest for executive union offices and by failure in other ways to direct the activities of the members under the force of the union's machinery—for example, by penetration and infiltration tactics, and formation of 'cells' or pressure groups within the union—it usually attempts to obtain a control of the shop committee or committees as a means of furthering its aims. As, however, the shop committees are usually constituted of shop stewards, a preliminary step is the securing of shop stewardships for persons of their own way of thinking. The shop committee then, particularly where the stewards who comprise it do not belong to the one union, is a generally accepted alternative by which the Communists hope to attain their objectives through the action of the workers where officials in the unions are hostile or unsympathetic, and composite union policy in the country is not in accordance with their designs.[4] L. L. Sharkey, General Secretary of the Communist Party in Australia, said:

The shop committees play a most important role in the preparation and mobilisation of the workers for strike action. They play an important role in leading the strike. . . In a revolutionary situation the shop committees would be one of the chief instruments for drawing

unions are won over', wrote Josif Stalin, *Works* (Moscow, 1954), vol. v, p. 56; but, he said, 'Formally, the Party cannot give the trade unions any directives; but the Party gives directives to the Communists who work in the trade unions', ibid., vol. x, p. 108. Both these passages are quoted by T. T. Hammond in *Lenin on Trade Unions and Revolution* (New York, 1957), pp. 3, 73. On p. 3, Mr Hammond observes that trade unions are the 'largest and most common organisations of the proletariat, and hence they are natural targets for Communist attempts at penetration and domination'. See also ibid., p. 125; and Isaac Deutscher, *Soviet Trade Unions* (London, 1950), chapter i.
    [3] See p. 11.
    [4] For the pressure that a number of semi-independent English shop stewards organizations endeavour to apply to official trade union leaders in furtherance of political considerations, see B. C. Roberts (ed.), *Industrial Relations: Contemporary Problems and Perspectives* (London, 1962), pp. 6, 7.

the whole of the working-class into the fight, into the street, and the general revolutionary struggle. After the taking of political power by the workers, the shop committee's role is again extraordinarily important. The shop committees, together with the Party branch in the factories, realize workers' control of industry; they lead the work of economic reconstruction and the raising of the level of socialist production in the work-places. . . The shop committee movement in Australia was weak and has only really commenced to grow under the influence of our Party.[5]

An additional agency, to which the Communists have turned in order to achieve their aims, is the 'shop area committee' or 'area committee' (the descriptions by which it is commonly known in Australia and in other places). This is a variation or extension of the multi-union shop committee, as it may be contemplated, in that it is not confined, in its identity or association, to a single plant or establishment in a locality as in the case of the normal shop committee, but is related, in its coverage, to more or all of the establishments and their branches in an industry or even to a number of industries spread or dispersed over a neighbourhood or region, quite irrespective of the character of the industries or the occupations of the members of the unions involved. It is little wonder that many unions regard, with more than a passing disfavour or suspicion, the existence and activities of shop committees, notably those where all of the members do not represent the same union, and shop area committees—especially those that cast their nets wide so as to comprehend, for their purposes, as many industries and occupations in a locality as possible.[6]

[5] *The Trade Unions* (Sydney, 4th ed., rev., 1961), p. 39. In the 19th Party Congress Resolution there is an instruction that the trade unions are to be 'strengthened by extensive job organizations, i.e., job stewards, shop committees and where practicable councils of shop committees'; quoted by J. Hartley in an article in the *Communist Review* (Sydney), no. 255 (March 1963), p. 89.

[6] There is a small pamphlet, in the nature of a comment on the aims and strategy of the Communist Party in Australia, that, allowing for the fact that it is now in some respects out of date, may be recommended as perhaps the most informative short exposition available to the general reader of the objects and actional methods of this party with respect to the trade unions. It was written by J. P. Maynes, Federal President of the Federated Clerks' Union of Australia, under the title *Conquest by Stealth* (Melbourne), and is expressive of a trade union point of view. The date of publication is not disclosed on the face of the pamphlet, but its first appearance was probably early in 1961.

Sino-Soviet Ideological and Other Divergences

The division that opened up in the ranks of the Communist
international movement, some little time back, through the reve-
lation of serious differences of opinion between Soviet and
Chinese leaders concerning basic ideological concepts and the
practical methods for the realization of the Communist objective, has had its repercussions in Australia.[7] These differences,
however, do not seem likely to bring about any alterations of
consequence in the role cast for the trade unions (including
the part allocated for shop committees and holders of offices and
positions in the unions), as laid down in the propaganda writings
of Lenin and Stalin and others of their school, for purposes of
the Communist quest for universal domination. In regard to
Australia there certainly are not discernible any such changes,
as far as can be ascertained from present-day publications emanating from Communist sources, or written under Communist
inspiration. Thus J. R. Hughes, in an article contributed to the
Communist Review, describes the affiliated trade unions as the
'main base of the A.L.P.'[8]—a fact, he insists, that is never to be
'overlooked by them as each campaign issue arises in the ranks'
—and says that the unions should 'on a daily basis exercise their
affiliation to the A.L.P. to pursue policies which strongly reflect

7 The Communist Party in Australia adheres to the Soviet viewpoints in
the controversy, and has expelled from its membership a number of persons
who expressed their dissent, while others who disagreed have resigned from
the party of their own accord. It has been suggested that those who favour,
or sympathize with, the Chinese opinions on doctrine and technique of
enforcement will eventually form a completely independent Communist party
in Australia for the spread of these views. As a matter of fact, so much has
been effected in realization of this design as to make it by no means an
exaggeration to say that the task, in its essentials, has now been accomplished. The situation that has thus evolved in Australia from the Sino-
Soviet ideological cleavage calls to mind, by way of contrast, developments
in Japan that have derived from the same origin. There a majority of the
members of organized Communism support, and have adopted, the main
Chinese assertions in the disputations, and events point to the establishment by the dissident minority and their connections of a separate Communist party in that country directed to the popularization of the Soviet
argument on the issues involved. In another case of close interest to Australia
where a division along the same ideological lines has occurred, in India, the
Soviet element is predominant, with the pro-Chinese rejects and withdrawals
bent, it would seem, on the founding of a distinct Communist organization
under their own control in that country.

8 A.L.P. is the generally accepted abbreviation for Australian Labor Party.
This organization is the principal representative of, and the chief spokesman
for, political labour opinion in this country.

the needs and desires of their membership'.⁹ Some of the policy
decisions of the A.L.P., arrived at as the result of deliberations
at recent federal conferences in particular, are manifestly un-
certain and vague in their expression and capable of more than
one meaning. Opportunities arise for decisions of this nature
to be construed for the advancement of the Communist intentions, or, for that matter, of course, in the interests of any association teaching other doctrines or principles. Mr Hughes, indeed, thinks that many of these decisions of the A.L.P. 'reflected
the inner conflict in the party and emerged full of ambiguity
and contradiction'—a circumstance, he would remind his readers,
that enables party members and the movement to 'take their pick
as to which interpretation of the various decisions can be applied'.¹⁰ In a context such as this, where a document lends
itself to an alternative construction that may be turned to the
advantage of a party, or made to suit its ends, Mr Hughes could
draw fresh attention to the 'need for consistent work in the
trade unions and on the jobs, to the involvement of the rank
and file workers in the progressive policies that are to be found
in great profusion in the numerous decisions of the A.L.P.'.¹¹
A heavy responsibility, he believes, rests with the affiliated
unions to publicize the positive points of the conference resolutions throughout the jobs, in order that this information can
become the 'property of the workers and strengthen unity among
them'. It is, he continues, 'important for the unions and the
workers to place a proper working class interpretation' on the
decisions adopted by the A.L.P.¹² Much depends, he thinks,
upon the degree to which the affiliated unions can mobilize the
workers, and succeed in developing a mass unity among the
people in support of any action deemed desirable to give effect
to the policy decisions.¹³

⁹ See issue no. 261 (September 1963), p. 293. Mr Hughes is a member
of the Central Committee of the Communist Party in Australia, and one
of the most influential figures in the Communist movement in this country,
in both its speculative and activist aspects.
¹⁰ See his article in the *Communist Review*, no. 262 (October 1963),
p. 318.
¹¹ *Communist Review*, no. 261 (September 1963), p. 293.
¹² *Communist Review*, no. 262 (October 1963), p. 321.
¹³ Ibid., p. 319.

NOTE TO THE CHAPTER

The Organizership in a Registered Organization

With the exception of the organizership, the superior posts
specified in this chapter are, in so far as they are related to a
trade union or branch of a trade union registered as an organization under the Act,[14] denoted in section 4(1) of the Act as
constituting 'offices' within the meaning, and for the purposes,
of that legislation.[15] The position of organizer as created by the
rules of most of the important registered organizations would
appear, however, also to fall into that category.[16] In *Cameron
v. Australian Workers' Union* it certainly was held that organizers appointed in furtherance of the Rules of the Australian
Workers' Union—the largest of the Australian trade unions—
were merely employees, and not holders of an 'office' for purposes of the Act.[17] In a number of respects, however, the provisions in the rules of this union governing the position of organizer differ considerably from the corresponding provisions in
the rules of the generality of unions—for example, the provision
according to which branches might 'employ' organizers at any
time. Each case must be left to rest on its merits. In the particular instance, the rules of the organization concerned would have
to be scrutinized before it could be determined whether the
legal tests and requirements essential to recognition of the organizership as an office were satisfied.[18]

14 See p. 2.
15 The 'vigilance officer' of the Waterside Workers' Federation of Australia, and the 'vigilant officer' of the Seamen's Union of Australia, can be
taken as the practical equivalent in function of the 'organizer' under the
rules of the generality of trade unions in Australia. In other days the 'roving
delegate', as he was commonly designated, had much the same duties to
perform as the 'organizer' of the present day.
16 Thus, in *Re Elections for Offices in Amalgamated Engineering Union
(Australian Section)* (1961) 3 F.L.R. 63, it was held that a divisional organizer
appointed under the rules of this union was the holder of an office in terms
of the sub-section.
17 (1959) 2 F.L.R. 45.
18 See, further, the discussion on pp. 11-14.

Part I

2

THE NATURE AND FUNCTION OF THE
SHOP STEWARDSHIP

Dual Function of the Registered Trade Union

The trade union, in the generally accepted use of the term, is a voluntary association established by, and for the benefit of, a particular class or aggregate of workers. It is constituted of the workers in question and is representative of them, and it owes nothing for its creation to statutory authority or design. These bodies can aptly be described in relation to their function, as they have been by W. D. Ross, as the 'natural custodians of the liberties of the working class'.[1] In most progressive countries legislation has recognized their existence, and approved the fundamental purposes for which they have been formed, besides conceding to them the right to exercise powers of a definite and substantial kind. In Australia, however, a trade union, when registered as an organization or industrial union under industrial arbitration legislation, federal or State, enjoys as a consequence a corporate existence and is endowed by that legislation with additional specific rights and powers of an important character. Such registration involves, at the same time, important specific duties and obligations, the responsibility for the fulfilment or observance of which is to the Commonwealth or appropriate State, as the case may be. From being in the nature of a legalized social and economic grouping of employees, equipped with a measure of authority, the trade union registered under Australian industrial arbitration legislation becomes, particularly by reason of a personified identity, a public institution as well, and its responsibilities are no longer limited in the main to its own

[1] See his article, 'Industrial Relations in Great Britain', *Law Quarterly Review*, vol. 58, no. 230 (1942), p. 190.

members or its own people. One result is that its prominence in
the community is considerably enhanced, as is that of those
persons who hold offices or positions under the administrative
arrangements for the discharge of the double function of the
registered organization or industrial union.

The new responsibilities have no historical or strictly logical
connection with the responsibility to its members or people, and
there is no inevitable or necessary relationship of significance
between the public and private functions of the registered organization or industrial union. The added responsibilities that accrue by virtue of the registration are related, in their essentials,
to the maintenance of the industrial peace of the country—as
distinct from the protection and furtherance of the special interests of the workers, the achievement of which was tradition-
ally the sole aim and object of the trade unions in other days
and the primary justification for their existence.[2] The great
majority of the trade unions of note in Australia are registered
under industrial arbitration legislation. The general effect is that
these unions, viewed as a composite entity, occupy a regular and
assured place among the institutions that constitute the basic
structure of Australian society, and that those charged with their
control and conduct administer a responsibility that is national
in its significance. On that account it cannot be other than
highly desirable that the ambit of their function should be
ascertainable with a measure of certainty—as in the case of instrumentalities vital in the Australian economy, such as the Commission, the various Commonwealth Banks under the statutory
arrangement, the Australian Loan Council and the Tariff Board
—enabling the function of the governmental authority of the
country to be exercised without embarrassment or apprehension
in the making of decisions of domestic application or external
significance, and the implementation of those decisions according to their tenor.

One manifestation of the new role of trade unionism in Australia is the growing interest shown by the community in the
policies of industrial labour, and the actions of its central and

[2] See O. de R. Foenander, *Trade Unionism in Australia* (Sydney, 1962),
p. 3.

local organizations in the carrying of these policies into effect. Another is the corresponding increase in the notice given by the press and other publicity factors to the decisions and activities of the trade unions, both individually and as collectively organized.[3]

Relationship of Shop Stewardship to an Office in a Registered Organization or Industrial Union

A. LEGISLATIVE DEFINITION OF 'OFFICE'

(i) The Commonwealth

Few will be disposed to dispute the remark of Lord Wright in *McMillan* v. *Guest* that 'office', because of the different meanings attributed to it in the various contexts in which it is used, is a word of 'indefinite content'.[4] In its relation to an organization or branch of an organization registered in pursuance of the Act, the expression is defined in section 4(1) of the Act to mean

(a) the office of a member of the committee of management of the organization or branch; (aa) the office of president, vice-president, secretary, assistant-secretary or other executive officer, by whatever name called, of the organization or branch; (b) the office of a person holding, whether as trustee or otherwise, property of the organization or branch, or property in which the organization or branch has any beneficial interest; and (c) every office within the organization or branch for the filling of which an election is conducted within the organization or branch.

For a fuller understanding of the implications of paragraphs (a), (aa) and (b), section 133 of the Act and regulation 115 (d) (i) of the Regulations promulgated under the Act (which provide for election by secret ballot in the case of offices specified in these paragraphs) must, however, be consulted. When, accordingly, the paragraphs are considered in conjunction with section 133 and the regulation, the drafting of the definition as

[3] Ibid., pp. 168-9.
[4] [1942] A.C., at 566; cf. his observation in a later case, *Aristoc Limited* v. *Rysta Limited* [1945] A.C., at 102, with reference to the word 'trade': ' "Trade" is a very wide term . . . Its great width of meaning and application can be seen by referring to the heading in the Oxford English Dictionary. But it must always be read in its context. That gives it the special connotation appropriate to the particular case.'

a whole nevertheless leaves much to be desired. It suffers, at the very least, from a measure of imprecision and suggests otiosity. Ambiguity is apparent when the dragnet paragraph (c) is examined side by side with the preceding particularizing paragraphs. The interpreter will, in all probability, feel the need for the exercise of latitude in his approach if he is to ascertain what is intended to be conveyed by the legislature in this paragraph. Indeed Dunphy J. in *Pegg* v. *Taylor*,[5] and in *Re Elections for Offices in Amalgamated Engineering Union (Australian Section)*,[6] insisted that it was 'impossible', in the circumstances, to read the paragraph literally, and in the latter case he mentioned two 'patent absurdities' which, in his view, would be the result of such a reading.[7] But regardless of what is said, in derogation or otherwise, of the definition in its express form, there can be no question that the meaning of the term 'office' under the statutory design, as the Full Bench of the High Court said in *Federated Ironworkers' Association of Australia* v. *The Commonwealth and Others*, is 'wide'.[8]

(ii) *The States*

In the industrial arbitration legislative measures of three of the States there are to be found definitions of the expression 'office' in terms similar to, or substantially identical with, those contained in section 4(1) of the Act. The various relevant sections are section 111 L of the Industrial Arbitration Act, 1940-1964 (New South Wales), section 5 of the Industrial Conciliation and Arbitration Acts, 1961-1963 (Queensland), and section 6 of the Industrial Arbitration Act, 1912-1963 (Western Australia). No definition of the term appears in the Industrial Code, 1920-1963 (South Australia), or in the Regulations and Rules of the Industrial Court of that State. The lengthy discussion by the Full Bench of the Industrial Commission of New South Wales in *Transport Workers' Union of Australia* v. *Knoblanche No. 2*[9] on the definition of 'office', adopted in the New South Wales measure in relation to industrial unions, is highly useful

5 (1959) 1 F.L.R., at 281-2.
6 (1961) 3 F.L.R., at 69.
7 Ibid.
8 (1951) 84 C.L.R., at 280.
9 (1954) 53 A.R. (N.S.W.) 501.

in the attempt to discover the meaning to be attached to this word under the verbiage of Australian industrial legislation.

There is an absence of industrial arbitration legislation on the statute books of the other Australian States—Victoria and Tasmania; the regulation of labour relations in these States is assigned to authorities whose methods are essentially legislative, as distinct from arbitral.

B.   LEGISLATIVE SILENCE ON THE DEFINITION OF 'SHOP STEWARD'

(i) *The Commonwealth*

The Act does not supply a definition of, or otherwise indicate a meaning for, the phrase 'shop steward', but there was no occasion for it to do so, since this legislation does not mention, or advert to, the expression in any of its provisions. It can, however, be taken that, in practice at least, persons so called in relation to an organization or branch registered under the Act are not within the scope of the statutory definition of 'office', and therefore not entitled, as holders of an office within the meaning of the Act, to the higher status and the increased powers and privileges that are conferred in terms of the rules of a normal organization, and accrue under the Act. The post that they occupy is not among those specifically named as an office in paragraphs (a), (aa) or (b), and in the usual case any election to fill it is purely a workshop or job proceeding, and not one 'conducted within the organization or branch' in accordance with the demand of paragraph (c). Even, however, if the rules of an organization that create its constitutional structure should provide for the election of shop or job stewards, at which all of the members of the organization, or branch, as the case may be, have the right to vote—a situation that could conceivably arise, especially in relation to a small organization or branch—the argument that a steward so elected has a valid claim to be recognized as the holder of an office would seem still to be insufficient.[10] It appears to be firmly established by the cases that the Court, to be satisfied, would require it to be shown, as well, that

---

[10] In *Pegg* v. *Taylor* (1959) 1 F.L.R., at 281-2, Dunphy J. said that the holding of an election by itself was not to be taken as an 'absolute test' in deciding whether a position is an office within the interpretation to be accorded to paragraph (c).

the position in question carries with it, under the rules of the organization, duties of a positive and substantive character—for example, involving a measure of executive or administrative responsibility—and that there is, incidental to it, an element of permanence to the extent that it will be occupied by a succession of persons from time to time, and not be subject to the termination of its existence on the death or retirement of a person holding it for the time being. English courts, in adjudicating on a claim for recognition of a position as an office, are accustomed to place great weight on the nature of the duties attaching to it, its continuity, and its independence of the persons who, one after another, fill it—an insistence that the position, in its actuality, is not classifiable as essentially subordinate, ephemeral or *ad hoc*.[11] The Australian judiciary, in dealing with issues concerned with the meaning of the word 'office', has usually been strongly influenced by these English cases, notably, perhaps, the decisions in *Great Western Railway Company* v. *Bater*,[12] *McMillan* v. *Guest*,[13] and *Mitchell and Edon* v. *Ross*.[14]

(ii) *The States*

There is an omission, too, of a definitive provision governing the meaning of the expression 'shop steward' in State legislation, that could be of service in guiding the tribunals in determining the relationship of the shop stewardship to an office in an industrial union. Having regard, however, to the fact that the definitions of the term 'office' in State and federal legislation approximate very closely, as pointed out, and that State as well as federal courts rely for assistance on relevant English decisions in their adjudications, it can be anticipated that the approach of

11 In *McMillan* v. *Guest* [1942] A.C., at 566, Lord Wright spoke of the word 'office' as a 'position or place to which certain duties are attached especially one of a more or less public character'; cf. the observation of Kelly C.J., in *Wool Selling Brokers Officers' Association of Australia* v. *Employers' Association of Wool Selling Brokers and Others* (1950) 67 C.A.R., at 227, where he points out that 'officer' is not to be used as a synonym for 'employee': 'The function of representation or agency, with usually the authority to make decisions in dealing with outsiders without reference of the transaction to superior direction, is the element in the position of an "officer" which, in whatever varying degrees, distinguishes it from that of a mere "employee".'
12 [1920] 3 K.B. 266; see particularly at 274 (per Rowlatt J.).
13 [1942] A.C. 561; see particularly at 564 (per Lord Atkin).
14 [1960] 1 Ch. 145; see particularly at 163-4 (per Upjohn J.).

the State tribunals in ruling as to this relationship will be much the same as that adopted by a federal court in a similar case.

C. THE PROBABLE CONCLUSION

There are no federal or State judicial decisions, known to the author, on the issue of whether or not a shop steward is the holder of an office. Bearing in mind, however, what has been said in these pages, a perusal of the contents of the remainder of this and the following chapter on the character of the shop stewardship will lead, it is suggested, to the conclusion that a claim for the identification of this position with an office under, or for the purposes of, federal or State industrial arbitration legislation will fail, save where the facts of the case are exceptional. This conclusion might find support in the provisions of some of the awards, to the extent that they indicate the mind of the industrial tribunals on the relative standing and authority of shop stewards (or job delegates) and officers of a trade union. Two of these awards—one federal, and the other State—are now referred to.

Under clause 31 of the Waterside Workers' Award made by the Commission in 1960, a vigilance or other officer of the Waterside Workers' Federation of Australia is empowered to go on any wharf or ship where cargo is being handled, but he is forbidden while there present to interfere with operations being carried on, or direct, advise or encourage men to cease their work; an abuse of this right can result in a refusal on the part of the employer to allow the officer to continue in its exercise. A duty rests on the officer, following observation or inquiries, to report any action believed by him to be in breach of the award, to make all complaints regarding the safety of methods employed, and to submit all claims for extra labour, to the foreman. Should he fail to obtain a satisfactory adjustment of any of these grievances, after conferring with the foreman or other representative of the employer, it devolves upon him to bring the matter, or matters, complained of before the appropriate Board of Reference appointed under the award, for hearing and decision.[15]

[15] A Board of Reference is an authority appointed for the purposes of an award, whose general function is to relieve the Commission of some of its less important duties. Section 50(1) of the Act empowers the Commission, by an award or by an order made on the application of an organization or person

On the other hand, the function of a job delegate who, as prescribed in the award, must be appointed at or prior to the commencement of each job from among the employees engaged on the job, is defined in the clause as 'spokesman for all the employees on the job in all matters arising between the employer and the employees'. The responsibility for directing the method of working at any job is declared to remain with the employer or his representative, with the job delegate enjoined not to interfere with the authority of the employer or his representative on the job.

Under clause 18 of the Metal Trades Construction (Alumina Refinery) Award made by the Court of Arbitration of Western Australia in 1962, the distinction is drawn between the respective jurisdictions of shop or job stewards and officers of an industrial union in the remedying of grievances and the settlement of disputes. The successive steps to be taken for the achievement of one or both of these objects are stated as follows: (a) discussion between the job steward on the site and the foreman on any matter that affects the workers concerned; (b) if the matter is not resolved as the result, further discussion between the job steward and the industrial officer or other officer nominated by the employer to deal with such matters on the site: (c) in the event of still another failure, the holding of discussions between representatives of the employer and union officers; and (d) where these methods have proved ineffective in producing agreement, a resort to a Board of Reference for a decision, provided that where such a Board would not be empowered to give a decision, reference to a higher authority as specified in the clause.[16]

Essential Function of the Shop Steward

The workers shop steward can be described as a member of a trade union appointed under its rules, whose function, broadly speaking, is to act as an intermediary between fellow members

bound by an award, to appoint or give power to appoint such a Board. See O. de R. Foenander, *Industrial Regulation in Australia* (Melbourne, 1947), pp. 28-30.

16 See *Western Australian Government Gazette*, no. 99, 7 December 1962. See also p. 72. Boards of Reference can be appointed for purposes of awards made under the Industrial Arbitration Act, 1912-1963 of Western Australia— see section 89.

of the union employed in a shop or department in an establishment on the one part, and the higher executive authority of the
union or employer management on the other. He is a means by
which the rank and file members of a union, distributed throughout the various scenes of employment in an industry to which
the union is by its constitution related, can be integrated more
closely within the union, and the strength and influence of the
union projected or elongated more fully into the workshops and
plant of an industrial establishment. Through him an additional
and an effective channel can be created by which the union as a
unit can be kept informed of what is taking place in these employments, and a useful method afforded by which union directives and requirements can be communicated to workers in the
various locations of employment in which the union has an immediate interest. By his agency, too, the workers are enabled
with expedition and convenience to convey their views on some
industrial matter to personnel of standing in the union, and to
make known to and to have discussed with management or its
representative 'on the spot', complaints and grievances that they
may be entertaining in regard to some of the details of their
jobs.[17] Unhappily there appears to be a tendency, in some
workers at least, to look upon the shop steward as a promoter
solely of their own interests, forgetting that the post connotes,
in principle, a double function and involves a divided loyalty,
a loyalty to union management as well as to fellow workers in
the shop (quite apart, of course, from the obligations of an employee to his employer).

The Twin Loyalties

The twofold responsibility of the shop steward, by virtue of
his position, has been adverted to by Australian industrial tribunals in language that can leave no room for doubt or misunderstanding. Thus, in *Electricity Commission of New South*

[17] In reference to Great Britain H. A. Clegg, A. J. Killick and Rex Adams,
*Trade Union Officers: A Study of Full Time Officers, Branch Secretaries and
Shop Stewards in British Trade Unions* (Oxford, 1961), p. 153, say: 'Our
definition of a shop steward is a local union representative who has definite
responsibility for the first stage of local negotiations, but is neither a full-time
officer nor a branch secretary with recognized negotiating rights in that
capacity.' This work is hereinafter referred to as H. A. Clegg *et al.*, *Trade
Union Officers.*

Wales v. *Federated Engine Drivers' and Firemen's Association of Australasia (Coast District) and Other Unions,* the Full Bench of the New South Wales Industrial Commission said that a 'shop steward appointed as such pursuant to the rules of the union is a representative of the union and not merely of the members of the union at the particular plant'.[18] Continuing, it reiterated and approved what it had observed in *In re Building Workers' Industrial Union of Australia, New South Wales Branch:*

The contention that a steward of this union on a job represents the members employed there rather than the union and that the union carries no responsibility for a steward's actions cannot be accepted for one moment. If a stoppage takes place, the duty of a member appointed or elected a shop steward is forthwith to advise the principal officers of the union of the exact position and of his own accord, and in co-operation with those officers, to take all reasonable and responsible steps to secure a speedy resumption of work.[19]

The apportioned loyalty that is incidental to the shop steward-ship can lead to difficulties when the respective claims upon its observance are not consistent with each other. Usually such difficulties are capable of solution without acerbity, as Australian experience would seem to indicate, by the display of tact and common sense on the part of those concerned. Pushed to extreme lengths, however, the conflict is capable of causing damage to union organization and prestige, and the common interests of the general body of members of the union. It is idle to deny that democracy in the shop, applied with wisdom and restraint, is highly desirable, but attempts at an autonomy in it that would reject the just and reasonable requirements of union management and administration have no justification, and are liable to be unfortunate in their consequences. Disputes between workers in a shop and the union executive are not infrequently before Australian industrial tribunals for settlement, but

18 (1956) 55 A.R. (N.S.W.), at 640.
19 (1954) 53 A.R. (N.S.W.), at 524. In *In re Dispute at Broken Hill Pty Co. Ltd Steel Works, Newcastle (No. 2)* (1961) 60 A.R. (N.S.W.), at 67, the Full Bench of the Industrial Commission of New South Wales recalled that it had pointed out that a delegate 'becomes, on his appointment as such, not only a representative of the members appointing him but a representative of the union'.

in the author's opinion these domestic squabbles, in almost every instance, have been in the nature of the evanescent, or the episodic, and in their passage have inflicted no lasting injury on Australian trade unionism. The hearing of one of these disputes before the Commonwealth Court of Conciliation and Arbitration revealed, in particular, how highly workers can be expected to prize their right, in terms of union rules or well-established custom, to elect the person of their choice to a shop stewardship.[20] In that case, *In the matter of the Federated Ironworkers' Association of Australia re Morts Dock Dispute,* the facts showed that acute opposition had been offered by branch members of the Association to the action of the National Council of the Association in removing an elected shop delegate from his position, replacing him by another person of its own preference, and that the controversy had developed into what was really a union faction fight waged with great bitterness and a considerable amount of personal asperity. As neither side showed any propensity to accept the assistance of the Court in its attempt to determine the dispute, O'Mara J. dismissed the matter and the dispute, without giving a decision on the merits of the issue.[21] The trouble was eventually settled and amity restored in the affairs of the Association, but only after a long struggle and with the assistance of the Australian Council of Trade Unions, whose intervention had been requested.[22] The dismissed delegate was installed in a position in another shop, while the vacant delegateship was filled by another person elected as the free choice of the workers.

Outlook for Disputes between Workers and Officials

It looks as if, in days to come, differences between workers in the shops and officials of the union will increase in number and variety, and possibly present more acute difficulties in their

[20] The right to elect shop stewards is generally appreciated by trade unionists; thus for France (*délégué du personnel*) see W. Galenson (ed.), *Comparative Labor Movements* (New York, 1952), pp. 341, 387.
[21] The proceedings in this interesting case were somewhat lengthy. See the Transcript of Proceedings, April-May 1945, and (1945) 54 C.A.R. 660, where the learned judge reported his decision to the above effect. See also pp. 31-6.
[22] For convenience, the Australian Council of Trade Unions is referred to hereinafter as the A.C.T.U.—an abbreviation in general use colloquially.

resolution. Automation processes and technological changes are strengthening their grip on industrial practice and production, while legislative provision for the education of the masses—wider in scope and higher in quality and standard—is becoming more generous, with opportunities for leisure made available for the workers in more ample measure through statutory action and award grant. The mechanical transformations in the mills and factories would seem to render imperative a closer concentration of control within the union, and a tightening of the authority of its superior personnel, if the organization is to continue to play its part as an effective force in the industrial environment. On the other hand, an outgrowth of the expanding educational developments and improvements in teaching resources and methods, accommodation, etc., in the schools and universities, and the availability of more spare time through the concession of a reduced ordinary working week, longer annual leave without deduction of pay, and so on, should be the unleashing of new forces and impulses of an explosive character in the minds of the rank and file members of the union, and these are calculated to find an outlet in the vigorous assertion of opinions by these members, and an insistence upon a greater share in the making of union decisions governing matters that are of immediate concern to them. Furthermore, the bonds of comradeship and the ties of common interests in the shop are still unifying to an extent sufficient to ensure that all operatives in the shop will continue to join in applying pressure on the full union to heed the views of a section of these operatives, even though there may not be complete agreement throughout the shop on the issue, or issues, in question.

Nevertheless, the amicable settlement within a reasonable time of intra-union controversies arising out of divergences of opinion on shop issues, except perhaps in the extreme or thorniest of cases, should not prove to be beyond the resources of prudence, tact and ingenuity resident in the union where it is soundly constituted. There would appear to be little cause to imagine otherwise, even with regard to situations where workers in more than one of the shops in which the union can exercise a jurisdiction combine and co-operate in the demanding of changes; for example, in relation to matters such as the allow-

ance of more latitude, or authority, to shop stewards in negotiation with the representatives of the employers, the grant of
payments on a higher scale to these persons in return for their
services, and an alteration in the conditions governing eligibility
for appointment to the position of shop steward and the tenure
of the position. With the passing of the years evidence has accumulated to show that those charged with the direction of the
affairs of the majority, at least, of the Australian trade unions
are capable and experienced men.[23] There is, moreover, little
ground for disbelief that this quality of competence will be
heightened as the result of the educational reforms alluded to,
along with changes that are in prospect in terms of the programmes of Australian trade unionism and the Workers' Educational Movement—*inter alia,* the adoption of more ambitious
courses for formal studies and training curricula within the individual unions and the Victorian Labor College, and the establishment of labour colleges in the States in which they have not
already made their appearance.[24] The impact of these movements in the educational field should be soon felt, and in an
appreciable measure. Statistics of age-groups, compiled from the
most recent of the census undertakings in Australia, reveal that
approximately one-half of the population of the country are
under thirty years of age, and from the evidence to hand the
trend of this proportion figure is pointing upwards.[25]

As regards the increased funds appropriated to public education, it can confidently be expected that those in whom the responsibility for the actual expenditure is vested will be not for-
getful of the claim for sound training of trade union personnel,
including shop stewards, whose role in the factories, in the com-
mercial establishments and on the job sites bids fair to grow
steadily in importance. The trade unions themselves, as in the
case of the corresponding organizations in other progressive
democratic societies, are in many ways conscious of the importance of disciplined and intelligent thinking on the part of those
in whom the administration of their business is located, if the
social and industrial changes that inevitably accompany techno-

[23] See O. de R. Foenander, *Trade Unionism in Australia,* p. 26.
[24] See pp. 36-7.
[25] See Census of the Commonwealth, 30 June 1961, *Census Bulletin No.
35* (Canberra, 1961).

logical innovation are to be understood, and the effectiveness of the power and influence that these bodies are enabled to wield in the life of the community is to be fully maintained. More particularly, there seems to be abundant promise that the trade union and labour collegiate standard courses of instruction will continue to proceed beyond a more or less elementary treatment of subjects that may, in some sense, be regarded as of immediate interest to a trade union in question, or Australian trade unionism as a collective unit—for example, the history, objects, internal organization, method of administration, and rights and obligations under the general and industrial law of these bodies singly, or as members of an association comprising those of them with common or similar employment interests, or more fully, as affiliates with the A.C.T.U. The development of these studies, it is hoped, will extend beyond subjects dealing mainly with trade unionism and the law directly affecting it to embrace, as in the case of trade union education in the United States, matters of broad human, national and international significance, so that trainees, besides being endowed with a fund of information of a useful kind, would be made capable of reaching judgments and well-balanced assessments on problems of the day.

All in all, under the influence of the progress in the field of education that is reasonably to be expected and the undisguised interest of trade union authorities and members in such advances, a series of events characterized by the exacerbation, recrimination and lengthy duration that distinguished the clash between the National Council of the Federated Ironworkers' Association of Australia and members of the Balmain Branch of the Association over the years 1945-7 is, in the author's opinion, scarcely likely to recur.

Behaviour

Possibly over-impressed by the support of fellow workers on occasions such as the Balmain affair, union representatives in the shops and on the jobs have at times betrayed an exaggerated notion of the nature of their post, and overreached themselves in the assertion of their supposed power. Attitudes of this character have a bearing on the rights of employers[26] as well as those

26 'It is in the interests of employers that stewards should represent their

of unions, and they have evoked the strong disapprobation of the industrial tribunals. Thus Mr Senior Commissioner Chambers, a member of the Commission, in *Bernard Smith-McDonald v. Amalgamated Engineering Union (Australian Section) and Others,* said that it is 'undoubtedly true that shop stewards, alive to their real responsibilities, can be and are of value in assisting to remove difficulties but it is, unfortunately, equally true that at times they assume unto themselves a standing out of keeping with their first duty as employees'.[27] And, in *In the matter of World Services and Construction Co. Pty Ltd and Others v. Boilermakers' Society of Australia,* Mr Commissioner Hood of the same tribunal also adverted to the liberties taken by some shop stewards in regard to their function. While allowing that a 'responsible and properly informed job representative can be an acquisition to the union, employer and fellow employees', he denounced as 'false and disturbing' an impression entertained in various places that such a person is equipped with the authority of an officer of the union, and went to the extent of saying:

Job representatives have little power invested in them. Indeed, it is proper to say that a job representative is very largely limited to the role of discussing matters with his employer and to reporting the result of those discussions to his union's officer. He has no power, for example, to call a stop-work meeting. My experience is that a number of unnecessary stoppages have occurred simply because the job representative has not been properly instructed and/or he has arrogated to himself powers which are outside his authority.[28]

Nevertheless, it would be unjust not to allow that, in the main, Australian shop stewards have shown themselves to be readily responsive to what are conceived to be the legitimate demands of officers of their union, and that, acting in their capacity as individual representatives as distinct from that as members of a shop or area committee, it is exceptional to find

unions and the members of those unions effectively'—*Report of 95th Annual Trades Union Congress, 1963* (published by authority of the Congress and General Council, 1963), p. 191.

27 (1959) 91 C.A.R., at 513-14. As a result of legislation passed in 1956 the existence of the Commonwealth Court of Conciliation and Arbitration has become purely nominal, its jurisdiction in effect being shared between two new tribunals—the Commonwealth Conciliation and Arbitration Commission and the Commonwealth Industrial Court—on the basis of giving the conciliative and arbitral authority to the former and the judicial power to the latter.   28 (1961) 98 C.A.R., at 464.

them guilty of provoking or fomenting unofficial strikes or stoppages of work.[29] As a class they can fairly be said to have withstood the temptation to seek, or make, opportunities for the exercise of the increased power that has come within their grasp over the past quarter-century through a high level of factory employment, and the shortage of labour supplies, in the country. The instances, too, must be rare when, having engineered a strike or stoppage of work in the shop without union concurrence or other justification, causing a loss of earnings to their work-mates, they have callously abandoned the scene of their employment and gone to a totally different occupation, leaving the union to suffer the odium or discredit for what has happened. In these respects their record appears to compare more than favourably with that of holders of corresponding positions overseas—in Great Britain, for example. Thus H. A. Clegg *et al.* have written:

> shop stewards do, of course, present a number of serious problems in the British trade union movement. Their close connection with unofficial strikes has attracted much attention. Whether their activities are provided for in union rules or not, their relationship with their union causes trouble, and few unions can be satisfied that they have adequate control over their stewards. Similarly there is a difficulty in integrating the workshop activities of the stewards with the official national negotiating procedures of the major industries in which shop stewards are to be found.[30]

There is certainly nothing in Australian industrial history to compare with the 'shop stewards movement' (as it is called) in Great Britain during World War I and the years immediately following, which involved a series of industrial and political agitations and actions, strongly militant and left-wing in nature, and which were characterized by a defiance of the orthodox trade union executives and a determination to centre labour control in the workshops.[31]

[29] For an example of shop steward action in Australia, in the calling of a strike or work stoppage, see p. 92.   [30] *Trade Union Officers*, p. 224.
[31] See, particularly, G. D. H. Cole, *A Short History of the British Working-Class Movement, 1789-1947* (London, 1952), pp. 358-62; and Branko Pribićević, *The Shop Stewards Movement and Workers Control 1910-1922* (Oxford. 1959), chapters v and vi. Incidentally, there was no such misbehaviour in the British 'shop stewards movement' of World War II, the contrast in this respect with the predecessor being most marked; see G. D. H. Cole, op. cit., p. 457. During World War I many shop stewards 'assumed on their own initiative an undue authority . . . deferring less and less to the trade

Mr Justice Gallagher on the Function of a Job Delegate

In a proceeding before the Commission Mr Justice Gallagher, one of its deputy presidents, made some interesting observations, somewhat in the nature of a homily, on how the function of a job delegate should be contemplated and the manner in which it should be fulfilled.[32] He was dealing with an appeal by an aggrieved job delegate, the working representative of the Waterside Workers' Federation of Australia and employed on the ship, *Tungus*, while the vessel was discharging cargo at her berth at Port Melbourne, against the cancellation of his registration as a waterside worker under the Stevedoring Industry Act, 1956-1963, by the Australian Stevedoring Industry Authority, on account of his conduct during the course of the unloading.[33] Registration of a person under this legislation enables him to qualify for engagement as a waterside worker for work on a wharf, or ship, at a port at which a register of waterside workers is established. One of the findings of the learned justice at the hearing was that the appellant had acted 'in gross abuse of his rights as a job delegate'. Another was that he had acted in 'direct conflict' with clause 31(b) of the Waterside Workers' Award, 1960, which imposes a duty on a job delegate not to interfere with the authority of the employer or his representative on the job.[34]

In announcing that the order of the Commission was that the appeal be dismissed Mr Justice Gallagher said:

In employer-employee relationships both parties have their rights and it is entirely proper there should be available, subject to the control, supervision and direction of the union, duly elected representatives of the men capable of exercising and recognized as having the function of safeguarding their interests. In the stevedoring industry particularly the nature of the work and the conditions under which it

---

unions of which they were nominally the delegates'; see D. F. MacDonald, *The State and the Trade Unions* (London, 1960), pp. 88-9; V. L. Allen, *Trade Unions and the Government* (London, 1960), pp. 130, 141-2, 150; R. M. Rayner, *The Story of Trade Unionism* (London, 1929), pp. 159, 222-3; and Arthur M. Ross in *Industrial Relations*, vol. 2, no. 2 (February 1963), pp. 74-5. See also pp. 37-8.

[32] Mr Justice Gallagher was the presidential member of the Commission assigned to exercise the powers of that tribunal in relation to the stevedoring industry, in pursuance of section 84 of the Act.

[33] *In the matter of an appeal under section 37 of the Stevedoring Industry Act 1956-1963 by L. Hillier against cancellation of registration as a waterside worker in the port of Melbourne* (1964), not reported.

[34] See p. 16.

is performed appear to make it necessary that there should be a system of job delegates. The job delegate is entitled to reasonable latitude and should not be prejudiced or harassed in his employment because of his activities . . . Let the job delegate be forthright in the defence of his mates. Concede to him the right to speak freely and without fear. Make allowance for the traditional militancy of the industry. But do not attempt to maintain that a job delegate may place himself outside the law, act in gross abuse of his rights, and at the same time claim immunity from his wrongdoing.[35]

In *In re Dispute at Broken Hill Pty Co. Ltd Steel Works, Newcastle (No. 2)*, the Full Bench of the Industrial Commission of New South Wales, too, said that 'while this Commission will be vigilant to protect the position of any delegate unjustly dealt with by an employer for legitimate activity on behalf of his union, it certainly will not regard delegateship as a magic cloak conferring on the wearer immunity from liability for wrongful actions'. An award, it went on to explain, 'confers rights on a delegate on the footing that the delegate will act in conformity with the responsibilities which his union has elected to bear by virtue of obtaining registration as an industrial union', and these responsibilities, it continued, 'include the obligation to have industrial disputes settled by resort to constitutional processes and not by direct action or job control'.[36]

Attitude of Employers towards the Shop Steward

Dealing with conditions in Great Britain, H. A. Clegg *et al.* have expressed the opinion that, on the evidence available, the authority of shop stewards in the factory has been 'fostered by management'.[37] Much the same can be said with respect to the treatment accorded to these persons by entrepreneurs in Australia. Briefly stated, the attitude of employers in this country

---

[35] The provisions of an award made by the Commission are part of the law of the Commonwealth, so that a breach or non-observance of any of these provisions constitutes a breach or non-observance of federal law, as the case may be. See the joint judgment of Isaacs C.J. and Starke J. in *Ex parte McLean* (1930) 43 C.L.R., at 479; and O. de R. Foenander, *Industrial Regulation in Australia*, p. 41.   [36] (1961) 60 A.R. (N.S.W.), at 66-7.
[37] *Trade Union Officers*, p. 181. 'Although there was some opposition . . . to their activities in earlier years, shop stewards are now generally accepted by employers—and in some cases formally recognized by them—as the union's accredited representatives and spokesmen for workers in the shop'—*Ministry of Labour, Industrial Relations Handbook* (London, rev. ed., 1961), p. 124. See also Arthur Marsh, *Managers and Shop Stewards* (London, 1963), pp. 9, 10, 25-9.

is, on the whole, to regard the shop steward as helpful in industry as a point of speedy and easy contact with workers—realizing that it is impracticable for union officials to be constantly 'on the spot' to represent and speak for employees in matters requiring immediate attention—and as useful because of the sound advice that, in ordinary circumstances, he can be relied upon to impart to fellow workers in the discussion of employment grievances. On that account, quite apart from the case where, under the provisions of an award, they are bound to recognize the union accreditation of a shop steward as such in the establishment,[38] employers can, by and large, be said to be prepared fully to support these persons in the exercise of any authority properly vested in them in pursuance of the rules of their organization.[39]

There will be little disagreement from management, or workers, with the views expressed in a testification of the Food Preservers' Union of Australia (Victorian branch) to the regard in which the shop steward is held on both sides in industry in Australia. The tribute is couched in the following language:

> To the boss he is generally looked upon with respect, as he knows that here is the man who has the loyal support of the majority of the men he represents. To the Union official he is a Godsend, for the steward is the backbone and pulse of the whole organization, and without him the Trade Union Movement would be operating in a vacuum.[40]

The Costain Case

A log of claims compiled by the Building Workers' Industrial Union of Australia following upon its re-registration as an organization of employees under the Act,[41] and served on a number of employers, contained a demand in terms of which (a) an employee who had been appointed union steward at a place of work, upon notification of that fact to an employer, should be recognized by the employer as the accredited representative of

38 See pp. 67-9.
39 For the view of employers on the function of job delegates on the waterfront, and its exercise, see p. 39.
40 See the *Food Preserver* (the official organ of the Victorian branch of the union), vol. 2, no. 8 (February 1964), p. 16.
41 The registration of this union was cancelled in 1948, and in 1963 the union was re-admitted to the register of organizations, and status, under the Act.

the union; and (b) such an employee should be allowed all necessary time during the working hours without deduction of pay to interview the employer, or his representative, on any matter affecting employees on the job, and such time as is reasonably necessary to interview members of the union, actual or prospective.[42] The award based on this log was made by the Commission by consent of the union and the employers, but the provision in it governing the right of a union steward to interview was restricted to meetings with employers or their representatives, and did not extend, in its coverage, to members of the union, actual or prospective.[43]

In what may, for convenience, be referred to as the *Costain Case*, stemming shortly afterwards from a notification under section 28 of the Act of a 'situation re Costain (Aust.) Pty. Ltd. and another likely to give rise to an industrial dispute',[44] it was alleged that a job steward of this union employed by the company as a carpenter, over the period of his employment with the company and particularly during recent weeks, had unduly interfered with the work being carried on by the company as the principal contractor on a certain building construction job, and similarly with the operations of a sub-contractor engaged in work on the same job site. The result, it was claimed, was the prevalence of discontent in employees throughout the building site on which the job was located.[45] The workers in the employment of the sub-contractor, it should be added, belonged for the most part to another trade union, the Amalgamated Society of Carpenters and Joiners of Australia. The company had expressed dissatisfaction with the amount of time spent by the job steward in question about the site during employment time, but away

[42] The demand is incorporated as clause 31 of the log (p. 14).
[43] The new award is known as the Carpenters and Joiners Award, 1964, and it embodies in its provisions clause 41 of the Carpenters and Joiners Award, 1962. This is the clause concerned with the right to interview accorded to job stewards; it limits the scope of that right so that it relates to the employer or his representative, and no one else.
[44] The section provides, *inter alia,* that as soon as an organization or employer becomes aware of the existence of an industrial situation that is likely to give rise to an industrial dispute, the organization or employer, as the case may be, must forthwith notify a Commissioner, or the Industrial Registrar or a Deputy Industrial Registrar appointed under the Act, accordingly.
[45] *In the matter of Costain (Aust.) Pty Ltd and Another and the Building Workers' Industrial Union of Australia* (1964), not reported. The notification under the section was made by the Victorian Employers' Federation.

from the duties that, under instructions, he was obliged to perform in terms of his contract of employment. The steward admitted that he had exhausted approximately 20 per cent of his paid time on matters involved in the discharge of his union duties, attention to the welfare of members of the union on the job, and discussions and communications with his employer or his representative. On the estimate of the company management, however, the figure in this respect stood at something decidedly higher. In the opinion of Mr Commissioner Matthews, who dealt with the notification, the time so taken up was 'quite considerable and above what might be regarded as fair and reasonable in normal circumstances'.

The Commissioner reminded the union that the award did not confer any authority for a job steward to occupy himself during working hours, without the permission of the management, in 'matters of union policy or objectives, or to concern himself with the employees of other employers', and warningly stated that a steward who exceeds his award rights 'should fully realize that he . . . places himself in jeopardy as to his employment'. It rests with him, the Commissioner went on to say, to refrain from devoting any of his paid time to the transaction of union affairs, however legitimate, that could 'properly' be undertaken in time that was entirely his own.

It was asserted, on behalf of the union, that some of the attention of the steward during his hours of employment was given to (a) a constant checking to make sure that no workmen were using Ramset guns (explosive-powered tools) other than those in possession of a licence under applicable State regulations, or who were trainees acting under the direct supervision of a certificated operator in accordance with the requirements of these regulations; (b) the keeping of a watch on the condition of the building scaffolding; and (c) the making of other precautionary observations and inspections in places where danger was believed to be latent. For an efficient prosecution of these activities, it was contended, it was essential for the steward to have regard to the conduct of operations of the men in the subcontractor's employment, as well as those in the employment of the contractor, seeing that a misuse or misapplication of certain types of tools, or the presence of faults or defects in the scaffolding, etc., constituted a threat to all employed on the site, irrespective of the employer by whom they were hired. In this context the Commissioner had these remarks to make:

The job steward concerned has, quite properly in one respect, deemed it within his province to ensure that safe working conditions apply in regard to employees of his employer, and certainly as to the operation of Ramset guns he has concerned himself to see that employees of the sub-contractor are properly authorized for this work because of the potential danger to all employees on the site. The one respect to which I referred as being proper, was his concern as such for safety. His duty under the award was to take up safety issues directly with his employer.

It is manifestly unreasonable not to concede that a job steward should have, and show, an interest in the personal safety of those whom he has been chosen to represent, and by virtue of his position be under an obligation of some character to protect these men against the hazards incidental to their occupation. Governmental authorities (central and local) in Australia and the generality of other industrialized countries have, of course, their set responsibilities in law to make provision for industrial safety, and to police the measures that are devised for this purpose. So also have employers. Nevertheless, there remains much that can be done by shop stewards and their kind in defence of workers against existing or possible dangers in employment, without encroaching on the function vested in these authorities or interfering with the discharge of the duties that attach to employers. Being 'on the spot' or close to the scene of operations, they enjoy special opportunities for noticing a breach or non-observance of the relevant regulations prescribed by the authorities, or structural flaws that may have developed about the job site; to the extent to which they report without delay what they have detected to their employers, they are able to make a contribution of no little value to the solution of the problem of safeguarding the lives and limbs of workers during the course of their employment. Industrial awards, perhaps, could be improved if they were to define, with as much fullness and precision as is practicable, the rights and duties of shop stewards in respect of the important subject of safety conditions that are to apply in the shops, and on the jobs.

NOTES TO THE CHAPTER

(1) *The Shop Steward Dispute in the Federated Ironworkers'*
Association of Australia, 1945-7

This dispute can be said to have had its origins—or at least to
have reached proportions of note—in the decision of the National
Council of the Federated Ironworkers' Association of Australia
to dismiss one of the members of the Association, a certain N.
Origlass, from his position of shop delegate in the boilershop at
Morts Dock & Engineering Co. Pty Ltd (an industrial establishment situated within the area covered by the Balmain
Branch of the Association). The ground was the 'attitude' of
and 'views expressed' by this member in relation to the affairs
of the Association. Mr Origlass was anti-Communist in his
opinions, and a man who had played a prominent part in union
politics; he had been elected to his position in the shop by fellow
employees in that shop. The dismissed delegate and his activities
had been 'investigated' by the Council, on a request to this end
that had been lodged by the officers of the Balmain Branch
of the Association. The resolution that led to the dismissal was
adopted unanimously, and was expressed in the following terms:

Moved Bro. Hopkins, seconded Bro. Wilson: That being of the
opinion that it is advisable to take the action hereinafter set out
because it deems such action necessary to ensure that a delegate of
the Balmain Branch of the Federated Ironworkers' Association of
Australia carries out the decisions and policy of the Union and
to secure the satisfactory working of the Balmain Branch of the
Federated Ironworkers' Association of Australia and to settle a dispute now in the Balmain Branch this Council:—Resolves to dismiss
Bro. N. Origlass from the position of shop steward in the Boilershop of Morts Dock & Engineering Co. Pty. Ltd. if he be still
validly appointed to that position and further resolves in view of
the attitude and views expressed by Bro. N. Origlass to inform the
Balmain Branch of the Federation and members of the Federation
employed at Morts Dock & Engineering Co. Pty. Ltd. that the
National Council determines that Bro. N. Origlass is not a suitable
person to be elected as such a delegate unless and until he gives
assurances satisfactory to this Council that he is ready and willing
to co-operate with the officers of the Union and to execute the
policy adopted by this Council or the National Conference; and
for purposes of permitting the consideration of such an assurance

if Bro. N. Origlass desires to offer the same, further resolves that Bro. N. Origlass be given reasonable notice of the time and place of holding the next meeting of the National Council to be held in Sydney in the month of June in order that he may attend the same for the purpose above mentioned.[46]

The generality of ironworkers in the shop protested strongly when Mr Origlass was formally dismissed, regarding the Council's step as an unwarranted interference with, and in fact an actual intrusion upon, a right of these workers, well entrenched by long practice, to choose their own representatives for the shop. The other delegates for the shop, two in number, resigned their positions as delegates in resentment at the action taken by the Council, intimating that they were unwilling to continue in the exercise of their union function without their colleague. The Council dealt with the situation by appointing three other persons to fill the vacancies—men known to be in sympathy with its policies and who favoured the decision to dismiss the delegate.

Thereupon members of the Association employed in the boilershop met, and it was agreed not to recognize the newly appointed delegates, and furthermore to make demands on the National officers that (a) these delegates should be removed from their positions within seven days; and (b) the predecessors of these delegates in the positions should be reinstated. The demands being ignored, all of the ironworkers engaged in the boilershop operations, except the newly appointed delegates, stopped work. Those who stayed on and were assigned to assist members of the Federated Engine Drivers' and Firemen's Association of Australasia in the shop were quickly in difficulties, because the latter refused to work with them. Members of the other metal trades unions employed in the shop adopted the same attitude as that taken up by the engine drivers and firemen, in particular, the Amalgamated Engineering Union (Australian Section) and the Boilermakers' Society of Australia.

The next stage of the clash was ushered in when a meeting of the Balmain Branch of the Association was held to consider the recent happenings at the Morts Dock site. The meeting, however, was terminated by the chairman—somewhat prema-

46 See Minutes of the National Council, 1943-51, pp. 117-18 (6 May 1945).

turely, it would appear—before anything of significance had been accomplished towards closing the breach in the ranks of the union, or determining any of the issues involved. The chairman, along with the other officials of the branch, was a firm supporter of the Council's attitude in the controversy, and allegations were made, from time to time, by some of the members that the ballots in 1944 at which these office-holders were returned had been rigged. A large majority of the members who had attended at the meeting remained behind, however, and resolved on another stoppage of work. Members of the Association employed in the shop at Cockatoo Docks & Engineering Co. Pty Ltd, and in the remainder of the shops located within the jurisdiction of the Balmain Branch, also met, endorsed a similar resolution, and accordingly ceased work as well.

The strike continued over a period of approximately five weeks, at the conclusion of which another meeting of the Balmain Branch was held, only to be closed for a second time by the order of the chairman, without results positive or of consequence having been realized. Again the men held their own meeting, and on this occasion voted the expulsion of the branch officials from office. Setting out to 'reform' matters at the branch they made fresh appointments to the vacated offices—among them Mr Origlass to the assistant-secretaryship—and the co-delegates at the boilershop who had resigned were re-elected to their old places.

Following this 'reconstruction' there was a general resumption of work without incident in the affected districts, but the new officials were able to settle down to the orderly performance of their duties only after some excitement, and a show of violence. Finding the door of the branch office barred against their entry they had it cut down; police action was invoked, and other premises had to be rented for purposes of administration. The Council, as was to be expected, repudiated the changes, refused recognition of the new officials, and declared the Balmain Branch to be closed. The supreme governing body of the Association, the National Conference, expelled a number of the leaders of the 'rebel' movement, including Mr Origlass, from membership of the Association.[47]

[47] The National Council is an executive, as distinct from a legislative,

For approximately two and a half years the defiance at Balmain of the Conference and the Council continued. At the expiration of that period the National Council officials sought the assistance of the A.C.T.U. in terminating the schism, and regaining for the Conference and the Council the control that had been lost. The request was granted, and this authority was able to effect a settlement on the basis of an amalgamation of the Balmain Branch with the Sydney Metropolitan Branch of the Association.[48] With this arrangement achieved a memorable chapter in the history of the union and, in fact, of the entire Australian trade union movement, was brought to an end. The shop delegates who had figured in the forefront of the conflict at the outset did not suffer, the co-delegates retaining their positions in the Morts Dock boilershop and Mr Origlass assuming a position in another waterfront shop.[49]

It seems reasonably clear from the evidence—particularly to the extent to which it is made available in the Minutes of the National Council, 1943-51—that a failure of the intervention of the A.C.T.U. at that juncture would have meant the lapse of some considerable time before a final agreement between the disputants, in liquidation of the troubles, could have been successfully negotiated. There certainly are strong grounds for believing that, at the time, little hope was entertained that this objective was attainable within a reasonable period as the outcome of informal conversations between officials and position-holders of the union, or the application of the machinery of the union to the solution of the problem as it had evolved.

In the ultimate result the central executive of the union, it will be seen, had the satisfaction of knowing that unity had been restored to the organization, and its own general authority revived and re-established in an area from which, for a protracted period, it had been completely excluded. On the other hand, the customary demand to select their own representatives by the members of the union employed in the shop had been fully vindicated, and their action in rejecting the persons imposed on them as delegates—unjustifiably in their view—had borne fruit.

authority, its general function being to ensure that decisions arrived at by the National Conference are enforced, and its will brought into effect.
[48] The amalgamation of the branches was effected in October 1947.
[49] See p. 19.

Moreover, it may reasonably be urged that the successful assertion of the local claim did not necessarily involve any real prejudice to an efficiency in its officers in the management of the business and the administration of the affairs of the union.

The developments that comprised this prolonged domestic struggle were punctuated by occurrences that must be regarded as, at the very least, distinctly arbitrary or irregular in character, and even, perhaps, as of dubious constitutional validity—to what extent and in what respects it is altogether difficult to speak with precision, seeing that the Rules of the Association in force at the time were in anything but a satisfactory state, in point of functional differentiation and location of powers within the union. The successive happenings attracted considerable attention throughout the community, the interest being by no means confined to union and other industrial circles, especially when the quarrel, limited in the early phases to workshop dimensions, had widened into a stern contest between rival groups for what was, in fact, the government of a branch of the Association.

It was only subsequent to the Council's action in dismissing the shop delegate that the Rules of the Association were altered to provide, in express terms, that shop delegates 'shall be elected at least annually . . . by the members at a meeting to be held on the job', with the reservation that where there was a failure by members to elect a delegate, a branch official was to appoint a delegate from amongst the members concerned. This provision now appears in rule 9 of the Branch Rules of the Association. Later amendments, too, clarified and strengthened the authority of the National Council in the control of persons holding office or position in the Association. At the time when the resolution for the removal of the shop delegate was voted, the Council was enabled, by virtue of rule 25(a) of the Federal Rules of the Association, to 'take such steps as it shall think fit to carry out all or any of the objects of the Association'. But, as the result of change (embodied in rule 19(1) (i) of the Federal Rules in their present form), it is empowered to 'Ensure that officers, committeemen, delegates, members and Branches carry out the rules, decisions, and *policy* of the Union' (author's italics). Moreover, a branch committee of management, under rule 9 of the current Branch Rules, is at liberty to withdraw its endorsement of an elected shop delegate if it be of the opinion, after inquiry, that the delegate has failed to carry out his duties in a satisfactory manner.[50]

(2) *The Victorian Labor College and the Adult Education Movement in Australia*

(a) *The Victorian Labor College*

Victoria is the only State in the Australian Commonwealth in which a labour college, or institution of a similar nature, has been established. The Victorian Labor College, as it is called, was founded in 1917, with a purpose declared to be that of 'independent Working Class Education'. The control of it is vested in a number of trade unions affiliated with it—forty-two all told—along with the Melbourne Trades Hall Council. Practically all of these unions have claims to be described as 'important', and include organizations interested in the heavy industries as well as those whose membership extends variously to transport and white collar workers. Its location is at the offices or premises of the Melbourne Trades Hall Council.

The Report of the Board of Management for the year ended 31 December 1963 complains of the 'small attendances' at the educational classes held, and laments the fact that the postal courses were 'slow in attracting students'; the latter courses, it averred, did not achieve the 'outstanding success we anticipated for 1963'. Attendance at the classes is entirely free, but a modest charge is made on those who take a course by post in order to cover costs and expenses—a charge that, it may be pointed out, is in most cases met by the trade union to which the interested or intending student belongs. The services of the tutors conducting the classes are purely voluntary. The main sources of financial support for the College are payments from the Trades Hall Council, income from the affiliation fees of trade unions and some assistance from donations. Lack of funds has apparently stood in the way of any substantial expansion and strengthening of the teaching activities of this institution, and its general progress.

---

[50] According to this rule, all shop delegates must be endorsed by the appropriate branch committee of management. See also p. 44.

The educational syllabus for the College set down for the year 1964 provided for lecture courses to be given in Australian History, History of the Labour Movement, Economics, Public Speaking and Industrial Law. Attention is drawn in the syllabus to the interest that the course in Industrial Law should have for trade union 'functionaries', and shop stewards.

(b) *The Adult Education Movement in Australia*

The adult education movement, which is active in all of the Australian States, in its teaching programmes also makes available courses and classes that deal with trade unionism in its various aspects, and kindred subjects. Under these auspices additional opportunities are at hand by which shop stewards and others with authority in a trade union—along with the generality of the members as well—are enabled to improve their knowledge and befit themselves for the discharge of union responsibility with which they are charged, or expect or hope to be charged. In at least one of the States, as a matter of fact, the Workers' Educational Association provides annual courses of study extending over a number of months, specially designed for, and directed to, the needs of shop stewards in carrying out their tasks. The duties regarded as incidental to the position of shop steward, the manner of establishing and maintaining contacts with fellow employees, the preparation of reports to be compiled, and the practice and procedure to be followed at workshop meetings are included in the matters and topics usually covered by these courses.

(3) *The Behaviour of Shop Stewards in Great Britain*

The relation of English shop stewards to strikes and work stoppages and their general behaviour in industry have been noted and considered by a number of writers. Their conclusions are by no means uniformly as unfavourable as that arrived at by H. A. Clegg *et al.*[51] Harry Welton, for example, believes that English shop stewards, for the most part, 'do a fine job',[52] and G. S. Walpole, who confesses that he had come to have 'considerable respect' for his own shop stewards, regards shop

[51] *Trade Union Officers*, p. 224. See also p. 24.
[52] *The Trade Unions, the Employers and the State* (London, 1960), p. 116.

stewards as the 'pivotal points of the opinion of organised labour'.[53] A Political and Economic Planning study admits that 'in some unions many stewards are favourably inclined towards the Communist Party and doubtless some are in most unions', but generalizing it claims: 'The normal steward is not as a rule out for prominence. He works hard, remains in office for long periods, understands the structure of his union and the procedures of his firm and industry, and his own part in both.'[54] Nancy Seear, too, says in much the same tone that 'there has been a tendency for a *relatively small* number of stewards to take the law into their own hands and to call an unofficial strike without the approval of the union and before the agreed procedure has been used'[55] (author's italics). She certainly adds, significantly, that the Trades Union Congress contemplated and assessed the situation as of such importance as to justify the authorization of a special investigation of the facts.[56]

(4) *A Recent Report on the Functions of Job Delegates*

In May 1963 a conference was convened by the Minister for Labour and National Service for the purpose of considering problems arising out of labour relationships in the stevedoring industry, particularly those with respect to continuity of operations in the loading and unloading of cargoes. Representatives from the A.C.T.U., Waterside Workers' Federation of Australia, employers in the stevedoring industry in Australia, Australian Stevedoring Industry Authority[57] and the Department of Labour

---

[53] *Management and Men* (London, 1945), p. 108.
[54] *British Trade Unionism—Six Studies* (Political and Economic Planning, London, July 1948), p. 131.
[55] In B. C. Roberts (ed.), *Industrial Relations: Contemporary Problems and Perspectives* (London, 1962), pp. 141-2.
[56] See K. G. J. C. Knowles, *Strikes—A Study in Industrial Conflict* (Oxford, 1952), pp. 37, 54; and *Report of Proceedings at the 92nd Annual Trades Union Congress, 1960* (published by authority of the Congress and General Council, 1960), p. 130.
[57] Powers are conferred, and duties imposed, under the Act and the Stevedoring Industry Act, 1956-1963, on the Australian Stevedoring Industry Authority with respect to certain matters in relation to, or affecting, labour employed on the waterfront. The function of the Authority is essentially inferior to that of the Commission (whose regulative jurisdiction over industrial relations extends to the waterfront as well as employments elsewhere), and may be regarded as adjunctive, or auxiliary, to that of the Commission. See O. de R. Foenander, *Industrial Conciliation and Arbitration in Australia* (Sydney, 1959), pp. 143-4.

and National Service attended. The conference appointed a small 'working party', as it was called, constituted of representatives of the employer and employee interests represented at the conference, the Authority and the Department, and instructed it to make a somewhat detailed examination of a number of specified matters, one of which was described as *Functions of job delegates on the job.* A report, unanimously agreed to, was prepared and submitted by the party to the conference after the lapse of approximately two months, and this in turn was referred by the conference to the consideration of the organizations of the employer and employee interests represented. The organizations endorsed the report, without modification or reservation.

The material part of the report dealing with the functions of job delegates on the job, contained in sections 6 and 7, is so brief as to enable it to be reproduced here in full without inconvenience. The sections are as follows:

6. Employers recognised that job delegates have an important function and a defined status in the industry. However, they consider that some delegates intrude into the areas of responsibility of foremen and supervisors, thus causing disputes. Moreover, on occasions, they act outside the status conferred upon them by the Award,[58] and pursue disruptive tactics which are not relevant to the working of the job in question. The Federation, however, maintains that there are supervisors and foremen who do not give job delegates due recognition and interfere with them in the carrying out of their duties. It also said that job delegates perform a valuable function within the industry.

7. The working party considered that there is some substance in both points of view and that there is an obligation on both sides to see that job delegates were allowed to function properly. Furthermore, the stevedoring industry has special features not ordinarily found in other industries which result in a lack of a stable relationship between supervision at the various levels and workers. This problem could be examined further under the item dealing with general organization of the industry.

The item, *General organization of the industry,* was another of the matters referred by the conference to the working party for investigation, but the party reported that, because of the limited time at its disposal before the date for the re-convening

[58] The award referred to is the award officially described as the Waterside Workers' Award, 1960. See also pp. 15-16.

of the conference to receive the report, it would be 'neither practicable nor useful to proceed with the discussion of this item which involves matters of such importance'.[59]

Attention may be drawn to the increasing influence, already of considerable proportions, that is exerted by waterside job delegates grouped in what are known as Job Delegates Associations in the framing of policies, and the making of decisions, by the respective branch executives of the Federation. These associations, each one of which comprises the delegates in a particular port, are located in the major Australian ports, and their influence is especially strong in the two most important, the ports of Sydney and of Melbourne. Part of the power that these associations are able to exercise is attributable, in no small measure, to the solidarity that characterizes their organization and the forcefulness that is a feature of their methods and their activities. Generally speaking, the views held by these delegates, and the aims for which they stand, are more to the left than those of members of the branch executives. In any study of employer-employee relations on the waterfront and the various problems to which these relations give rise, careful consideration should be forthcoming for the industrial and political ideas of these delegates, the interests that they are endeavouring to further, the extent to which the control and direction of the affairs of the Federation are affected by the strategy of the associations, and the effects of their operations on the industrial peace.

[59] The report has not been printed, and it is understood that there is no intention that it will be.

3

THE SIGNIFICANCE OF THE SHOP
STEWARD IN INDUSTRY

Other Titles

A number of Australian unions prefer to use, in their rules, an expression other than 'shop steward' to denote their representatives in the shops, factories, mills, yards or establishments, or on the jobs. Examples are: shop president (Australian Boot Trade Employees' Federation), steward or country agent (Australasian Society of Engineers), shop delegate (Federated Ironworkers' Association of Australia, and Boilermakers' Society of Australia), shed representative (Australian Workers' Union),[1] job steward (Amalgamated Society of Carpenters and Joiners of Australia—in respect of members working on temporary locations), lodge representative (Australian Coal and Shale Employees' Federation), job delegate (Australian Builders' Labourers' Federation,[2] Federated Ship Painters' and Dockers' Union of Australia, Waterside Workers' Federation of Australia, and Seamen's Union of Australia), and works representative (Australasian Meat Industry Employees' Union). In Australian usage 'steward' is in danger of being superseded by 'delegate' (colloquially, often 'delo') as the prevailing description of the union representative in the shop or other place to which his duties appertain, or in which they are performed. On the other hand 'shop steward' is the name 'in most common use' in Great Britain, although there are other titles as well by which shop representatives are widely known in that country.[3]

[1] The Australian Workers' Union Construction and Maintenance (Hydro-Electric Commission, Tasmania) Award, 1964, uses the expression, 'job representative', in reference to the representative appointed by members of the Australian Workers' Union employed on a job—see clause 54(b).

[2] Under the Rules of the Federation and of most of the other building unions in Australia, job delegates have been appointed to act 'in respect of more than one place or area'; the main reason is the intermittency that characterizes work performed in this industry.

[3] See *Report of Proceedings at the 92nd Annual Trades Union Congress*,

Eligibility for Appointment

In the usual case no qualification is demanded as a prerequisite
for the holding of a shop stewardship, beyond membership of
the union and employment in the relative shop. There is, however, an interesting provision in the Rules of the Amalgamated
Engineering Union (Australian Section),[4] according to which
adult membership of the union over a period of at least twelve
months is necessary for eligibility for the position.

Appointment

Whether shop stewards can, in fact, be appointed depends in
the ultimate analysis on the intendment, express or implied, of
the rules of the union in question. The courts have usually shown
a liberality in the construction of these rules, being disposed, in
the language of Mr Justice Isaacs, as he then was, in *Amalgamated Society of Engineers and Others* v. *Smith,* to read them

not as the strictly prepared and technically framed stipulations inserted in some legal instrument of lawyers, but as the plain and
business-like statement of members of the trades concerned, com-
bining for mutual support, and setting down the terms of their combination in language which is applicable to their situation and intended (subject to the presumptive intendment of legality) to be
understood apart from technical rules of interpretation.[5]

The method of appointment varies from union to union, and
again is determined in the last resort by the provisions of the
rules. In some instances, or in some circumstances, the appointment is made directly by the union, or the committee of management of the branch or district relevant to the locality in which
the shop to which the steward is to be attached is situated. In
most cases, however, the appointment is by way of formal con-
firmation by the executive of the union, or official acceptance or
ratification in some other shape, of the result of a vote taken

1960 (published by authority of the Congress and General Council, 1960),
p. 128.
    4 This union is hereinafter referred to as the A.E.U. It is the second largest
of the Australian trade unions, being exceeded in size of membership by the
Australian Workers' Union only, and is the largest trade union affiliated with
the A.C.T.U. So, too, the English Amalgamated Engineering Union is the
second largest of the trade unions located in Great Britain.
    5 (1913) 16 C.L.R., at 559. See also O. de R. Foenander, *Trade Unionism
in Australia* (Sydney, 1962), pp. 109-11.

among the members of the union employed in the shop or plant, or on the job;[6] thus, under the Rules of the A.E.U., shop stewards when elected must be approved by the appropriate district committee of the union, and pending that approval being given they have no authority to proceed to the exercise of the function. Under the rules of some unions acceptance of the position by the person appointed is compulsory, and in the case of the Federated Moulders' (Metals) Union of Australia, where a person so appointed refuses to carry out his duties he is to be dealt with in such manner as the appropriate State Executive Council of the union deems fit. There are instances, indeed, where under the rules each member employed in the shop is liable to be fined where there is a neglect to elect a shop steward in exercise of power granted by the rules. According to the Rules of the Federated Ironworkers' Association of Australia a branch official of the Association is obliged to appoint a shop delegate from among the members concerned, in the event of those members failing to elect one of themselves to the position, and for validity the delegate, whether elected or appointed, must be endorsed by the branch committee of management.[7]

Tenure

It is not possible to generalize, with any degree of satisfaction, as to the length of time for which a shop stewardship can be held. In a number of cases the tenure is for one year, with eligibility for reappointment, but there are instances (sometimes thanks to job custom) where the period is less; for example, three months for job delegates of the Federated Ship Painters' and

6 In terms of the Rules of the Australian Workers' Union there are two representatives at each shed—one is elected by the shearers as their representative, and the other is elected by the shed hands to represent them. As regards the Seamen's Union of Australia two job delegates are elected on each ship; one is the representative of the 'deck crew', i.e. seamen, A.B.'s, etc., and the other is the representative of the 'down below' men, i.e. greasers, firemen, etc.

7 H. A. Clegg et al., *Trade Union Officers* (Oxford, 1961), p. 162, say, in reference to Great Britain: 'Some union rules make no mention of shop stewards. Not all those which mention them prescribe the method of appointment, and those which do are far from precise.' In regard to the United States, Jack Barbash, *Labor's Grass Roots* (New York, 1961), p. 113, writes: 'The steward is usually elected by the workers in the unit which he represents. It is not rare, however, for the steward to be coopted by the local union officers.' See also Florence Peterson, *American Labor Unions* (New York, second rev. ed., 1963), pp. 76, 163.

Dockers' Union of Australia. With some unions the rules provide that a shop steward may be removed from his position at any time by resolution of the executive, and in terms of the rules of others the appointment is subject to termination at the discretion of the relevant branch committee of management. Under the Rules of the Federated Ironworkers' Association of Australia, power is vested in the appropriate branch committee of management to withdraw its endorsement of a shop delegate if satisfied, after investigation, that the delegate has failed to carry out his duties.

Remuneration

Shop stewards in a number of unions are entitled to remuneration for their services, and where this is forthcoming the question has usually been dealt with in the rules. For the most part the amount is purely nominal, representing little more than a token payment to compensate for fares, postages, telephone calls and other incidental expenses incurred, or loss of time involved. Sometimes the rules fix a sum or name a percentage commission on all moneys, for example, five, ten or even up to fifteen per cent in a few cases—with the exception, in a limited number of instances, of levies—which are collected by the shop steward from members, or which come from the proceeds of sales of membership tickets (for example, in a shearing shed under the Rules of the Australian Workers' Union), and duly paid in by him. In other cases they leave the rate or figure to be decided by an authority in the union (for example, the appropriate branch or divisional committee of management), or stipulate that a salary shall be determined by the union at specified intervals. Where no provision of any kind is made for payment a local levy is sometimes imposed as a gesture or mark of appreciation (for example, the A.E.U.). There are not a few unions in which the responsibility for collecting contributions from members rests with the branch secretary, but in no case known to the author is payment made to this officer as a return for the discharge of this duty. In accordance with some rules payments, too, are made to shop stewards for being present at meetings that, according to these rules, they are under an obligation to attend. Shearers have been known, on occasions, to collect for presentation to their shed representative a sum additional to that which the representative is entitled to receive under the rules of the union (the Australian Workers' Union). But there is no provision in the rules for such extra payments; these are purely *ex gratia* in nature, and a matter entirely within the discretion of the shearers concerned.

Assistance is available under the rules of some unions for the fulfilment of the shop stewardship function. Indeed, in the case of the Australian Workers' Union, it is mandatory upon members at a shearing shed to appoint two of their number to act as a committee to aid the shed representative in the carrying out of his duties. No payment can be claimed, under the rules, by a member for help thus rendered.

Most of those who contest the post of shop steward would, no doubt, regard the remuneration aspect as a secondary consideration, the true reward for the performance of the service in their eyes being, very probably, the assistance that can duly be expected in the realization of aspirations entertained for advancement to office in the union, or in the general trade union movement. This can be taken as the chief reason why, in the normal case, little difficulty has been encountered in filling these positions with suitable candidates. There is also the fact that tenure of the position, with some of the better conducted unions, can provide the opportunity for acquiring useful training and practical experience in administrative techniques, estimated to be not without advantage to a man with ambition.[8]

Rights and Duties

The duties and responsibilities cast on union representatives in the shops and on the jobs, and the rights and authorities at their

[8] In Great Britain it would appear that, for the most part, ordinary shop stewards do not receive payment, and that where payments are made the sum is 'small'; indeed, these stewards 'may lose money as a result of union work'; see H. A. Clegg et al., *Trade Union Officers*, p. 165. According to the *Ministry of Labour, Industrial Relations Handbook* (London, rev. ed., 1961), p. 124, the payments are 'generally not large'. See also H. A. Turner, *Trade Union Growth, Structure and Policy* (London, 1962), p. 284. As regards the United States, Jack Barbash, op. cit., p. 127, says that shop stewards are 'usually compensated (dues remission and/or a nominal fee) for their services but compensation is contingent on attendance at steward meetings and membership meetings'. Delbert C. Miller and William H. Form, *Industrial Sociology* (New York, 1951), p. 246, speak of the task of the shop steward as 'thankless'.

disposal, are not uniform throughout the unions, and the variation is as to both number and kind. In some cases the rules of the union set them out at length and in some detail, while in others a short statement in broad or concise terms is considered to be sufficient. To be informed of these powers and obligations it is sometimes not enough to rely on the express terms of the rules—whether as to the rules as a whole or in their context, or as to the clauses in the rules dealing specifically with these matters—and it may be necessary to learn what is implied in the language according to the interpretation and findings of courts of law, or domestic union tribunals, to ascertain the intentions of the makers of the rules.[9] There are instances, too, where tradition or long-standing practice in the conduct of the affairs of the union is accepted by members as the criterion for the exercise of authority by shop stewards or as justification for the tasks imposed on these persons, while in still other cases it seems to be allowed, by general consent or understanding, that the decision on such questions—perhaps in pursuance of some principle or doctrine of inherent power—lies within the discretion of some top union authority (that is, the committee of management of the union or of a branch). In many unions, by virtue of the terms of the rules or established practice, general control or supervision of the conduct of shop stewards in relation to the affairs of the union is entrusted to the relative district or branch committee of management, and in some cases the attendance of the shop steward at the ordinary general meeting of the committee is imperative. But no branch secretary or other authority of a union is at liberty to instruct a shop steward to do something that, under the rules of the union, it is the duty of the branch secretary himself, or other authority of the union, to perform. This is a situation in which the principle, known to lawyers as *delegatus non potest delegare,* can be said to apply.[10]

The following are among the better-known duties and powers imposed, or conferred, on Australian shop stewards:

(1) To collect or receive on behalf of the union contributions, subscriptions, fees, levies, dues, fines and other moneys owing and payable to the union or branch by fellow members in the

9 See O. de R. Foenander, *Trade Unionism in Australia,* pp. 122-4.
10 See the judgments of the Court in *Kidd* v. *Firth and Others* (1964), not reported.

shop, or other unit where they are employed; to issue receipts for these from a union duplicate receipt book provided for the purpose, or distribute official receipts for them as sent by the branch office; to enter details of these transactions in a cash book, and transmit the moneys to the secretary of the union or other authorized person within a specified time or times; and to examine periodically and sign the contribution cards of members of the union employed in the shop.

(2) To forward to the union at fixed intervals the names and current addresses of all members of the union employed in the shop, indicating the cases where members are not 'financial'; to make every effort to ensure that all persons starting work in the shop are duly qualified trade unionists; to interview non-members of the union employed in the shop and eligible for membership of the union, and 'beat them up' or endeavour otherwise to induce them to join the union, supplying applicants for membership with the prescribed forms; and to report to the union successes and failures in these recruiting operations, including the names of the workers interrogated or interviewed.

(3) On demand from the union at any time to account forthwith for all union books and funds held by them, and to produce or deliver these books and funds to the union within a specified time.

(4) To distribute on behalf of the union to members of the union employed in the shop, summonses, ballot papers and notices of any kind, and under the instructions of the union to disseminate information of any sort.

(5) To report to the union any infringement or non-observance of an industrial award, determination or agreement of which they are aware, or which they have reason to suspect has happened, or is happening, affecting the trade or calling in which members of the union employed in the shop are engaged.

(6) To use every endeavour to see that all who are employed in the shop are being paid at rates, and are working under conditions, approved by the union, and discharge their duties in compliance with the standards of the shop; with these objects in mind to scrutinize cards and pay tickets and notify the union of any case in which it is found that the position is not satisfactory, and which is not of a character that is rectifiable or properly

adjustable as purely a shop matter to be taken up with management.

(7) To keep the union regularly informed in regard to all matters and events connected with operations in the shop calculated to be of interest to it—for example, the existence and nature of any dispute, or the probability of any dispute, affecting work in the shop; details of accidents in the shop that have caused injury to members of the union during the course of their employment, and the presence of unguarded or otherwise dangerous machinery in the shop; and also particulars of a minor significance such as the date when shearing is to begin, or when it actually commenced, in a shed.

(8) To investigate complaints made by members of the union in relation to their employment in the shop, and where the occasion is deemed appropriate for shop steward action, to interview foremen or other representatives of management with a view to the satisfaction of these grievances and the removal of their causes.

(9) Generally to act as representative of the union in the shop where they are employed, and to watch over and protect the interests of the branch in that shop.[11]

Usual Duties

Of these duties it would appear that those involving, or connected with, the recovery and collection of payments owing by members of the union, the reporting of occurrences and developments of interest in the shop, and attention to the rights and grievances of members arising out of their jobs (including steps taken to secure managerial recognition of these rights, and correction or adjustment of these grievances), are the most usual ones prescribed. The procedure or practice known overseas as the 'check off'—an arrangement with the employer in accordance with which, subject to the worker's consent (expressed almost invariably in writing), contributions due by members to the union are regularly deducted from earnings envelopes and made

[11] In regard to Great Britain see H. A. Clegg *et al.*, *Trade Union Officers*, pp. 155, 181, 225; and V. L. Allen, *Power in Trade Unions*, pp. 39, 184. For the United States, see Florence Peterson, *American Labor Unions*, pp. 76, 163. See also *British Trade Unionism—Six Studies* (Political and Economic Planning, London, July 1948), pp. 128-30; and *Ministry of Labour, Industrial Relations Handbook*, pp. 10, 123-5.

payable direct to the union—is not as common in Australia as in the United States and other countries, but it is steadily gaining ground.[12] All things considered the collection of contributions must be assessed as occupying a comparatively minor place, in point of importance, in the catalogue of responsibilities of a shop steward in Australia, certainly with respect to the great majority of these persons. More weight is to be attached to the requirement to keep officers of the union informed of events and happenings in the shop, especially those of an industrial character. A very serious view is usually taken of lapses in this regard on the part of a shop steward, particularly where he does not notify the existence, or obvious imminence, of an industrial dispute, and the failure of his duty in this regard renders a shop steward, under the rules of some unions, liable to a fine (for example, the Australian Boot Trade Employees' Federation).

Clearly the main function of an Australian shop steward in the ordinary case is to conduct, as the chief representative of his union, negotiations with management covering matters of local shop import, such as special rates and special conditions of employment, including amenities. It is to matters such as these that, generally speaking, his role as a bargainer can be expected to be limited, with the distance to which he is entitled to proceed in the execution of this task carefully observed and severely circumscribed. Contrary to what is customary in countries like Great Britain where shop stewards determine or adjust, in discussions with management, rates to apply in furtherance of formulae and criteria expressed in the National Agreement, Australian shop stewards do not, to any extent, negotiate with employers on matters covered by, or connected with, the principal award or central agreement governing affairs in the industry. In the

---

[12] A provision in this respect governing contributions in the case of members of the Australian Workers' Union, employed in oil refining processes, is to be found in the A.W.U.—Queensland Oil Refineries Pty Ltd Award, clause 28 of which is as follows: 'The employer will accept orders by the employees to direct the employer to deduct the union dues in not more than two deductions per annum, and the employer shall pay to the authorized official of the Union the total amount so deducted.' The inclusion of a provision of this nature is eminently suitable to conditions in which an organization has a membership dispersed, or thinly scattered, over a wide area; the clause can prove highly useful and of considerable value in such circumstances, by reason of the economy that is possible in the demands made on the time necessary for collecting union contributions.

usual case they have no responsibilities in the fields of job evaluation, overtime schedules, time and motion studies and rate-fixing where workers are paid by results—areas in which shop stewards in other lands figure;[13] decisions on vital questions such as a stoppage of work, change in an industrial practice or alteration of an industrial principle, too, are not meant for them. Dealings of shop stewards with management can be generalized as not being of the same prominence, and not involving questions of consequence in the same degree, in Australia, as in the better-known overseas countries. In short, the function and standing of the shop stewardship in Australia, while far from negligible in point of importance or interest, and by no means to be brushed aside as not worthy of any close attention, are not of a significance equal to those attaching to the corresponding post in other industrialized countries.

An instance may be quoted of the limited extent to which shop stewards in Australia are permitted to proceed in negotiation, when differences have arisen with management. During June 1962 shop stewards representing the A.E.U. and the Australasian Society of Engineers complained to a representative of the De Havilland Aircraft Pty Ltd that five members of the Vehicle Builders Employees' Federation of Australia employed by the company were engaged on work which, they claimed, was within the province of members of their unions to the total exclusion of members of all other unions. All five persons in question were qualified tradesmen, two being employed in the classification of ground engineer and the remainder in the classification of inspector. No satisfaction attended the action of the stewards, whereupon officers of the unions stepped in and took charge of the situation. Organizers visited the plant, inspected the work in

13 Thus, as regards the United States Florence Peterson, *American Labor Unions*, p. 196, mentions job evaluation, work loads and plant rules as among the 'major' responsibilities of shop stewards in the field of internal shop activities. H. A. Clegg *et al.*, *Trade Union Officers*, pp. 155-6, point out, with respect to Great Britain, that in circumstances where workers are paid by results, shop stewards are 'likely to be involved in rate-fixing' in discussions with management to find an acceptable rate for each job. They are concerned also in this country with union demarcational matters and disputes, and negotiate special arrangements with respect to rates for shift, weekend and overtime work. See B. C. Roberts (ed.), *Industrial Relations: Contemporary Problems and Perspectives* (London, 1962), p. 139; and see also *Ministry of Labour, Industrial Relations Handbook*, p. 125.

question and made further inquiries. Following discussions with the union officers the company refused to accede in full to the union demands in relation to the allocation of the work, and lodged a notification under section 28 of the Act of the existence of an industrial dispute. The Commission duly intervened, and eventually determined the matter and the dispute.[14]

Nevertheless, within the sphere to which their dealings with employers are restricted, shop stewards have at times displayed amazing astuteness in discovering possibilities and opportunities for the framing of demands to the advantage of workers, and zeal combined with alertness in exploiting them to the full in the interests of these workers. A typical example is their activity in making claims for payments, over and above the ordinary rates prescribed for employment under awards (usually described industrially as 'allowances'), on the ground that the job in question is characterized by some special feature or incident—for example, an assertion that the job is performed in wet, damp, or unusually dirty, disagreeable, arduous or dangerous conditions, or at a height or on a platform, or in a tunnel or some confined space, or in circumstances or surroundings where the temperature is maintained by artificial means at a relatively high, or low, temperature.[15]

Embarrassment of Shop Stewards in the Discharge of Duties

The function of the shop steward is not always performed without the experiencing of serious embarrassment, and a sense of frustration, by the shop steward himself. There have been cases where these persons, called upon to remedy a complaint made by a worker in the shop, discover after careful inquiry that it has no foundation in fact, and the finding accordingly when communicated to the aggrieved worker has not always been received in the spirit of appreciation that it deserves. Sometimes relevant questions that a shop steward considers necessary to put to the complainant, in the course of the investigations, are regarded with resentment and even with anger. The zealous

---

[14] *In the matter of the Amalgamated Engineering Union (Australian Section), Australasian Society of Engineers and Vehicle Builders Employees' Federation of Australia re De Havilland Aircraft Pty Ltd* (1962) 100 C.A.R. 464 (Commissioner Apsey). See p. 28 in regard to section 28 of the Act.

[15] See O. de R. Foenander, *Industrial Regulation in Australia* (Melbourne, 1947), ch. XVII.

steward, indeed, stands in danger, at times, of being unfairly
stigmatized as a 'boss's man', and direct charges or cheap insinu-
ations to this effect can lose for him the confidence of those
whom he is supposed to represent and the popularity of those
on whose behalf he is expected to speak and act.

The shop steward, too, may at times find himself in difficulties when the shop is divided in opinion on the merits of some
employment issue or controversy, or even, perhaps, as regards a
purely personal difference involving groups of workers that has
arisen in the shop. He may feel himself impelled to support one
side, in accordance with the view that he has taken of the matter,
or he may adjudge it prudent or expedient, in the interests of
the workers concerned, to endeavour to settle the question on
the basis of a compromise of some sort. There is always the
danger that whatever decision he makes and whatever course he
adopts offence will be taken by a section of his fellow workers
in the shop, and that the trust and backing to which he is entitled as a union representative may, to that extent, be prejudiced.[16]

Mr Justice Nevile on the Authority of Shop Stewards

In timely and well-chosen language Mr Justice Nevile, in
*Coastal District Committee, Amalgamated Engineering Union
Association of Workers and Others* v. *Constructors John Brown
and Others,* drew the attention of shop stewards to the restricted
nature of their function, and the need for caution against the
exercise of authority in excess of that to which they are entitled.[17]
Some of these persons, he pointed out, seem to be guided in
their industrial actions solely by a desire to please their fellow
workers in the shop, in disregard of the fact that their powers are
limited by the rules of the union to which they belong, and by
any relevant provisions in the award governing the industry in
which they are employed. The learned justice advised, as a
means of familiarizing shop stewards with the nature and extent
of their powers, that each of them should be furnished with a
copy of the appropriate award. Reminding them that, in general,

16 See Burleigh B. Gardner and David G. Moore, *Human Relations in
Industry* (Chicago, rev. ed., 1950), pp. 133-4.
17 Mr Justice Nevile was President of the Court of Arbitration of Western
Australia.

the right of a shop steward to have discussions with the employer or his representative on the question of employment grievances, and other industrial affairs in the establishment, is confined to smallish matters of day-to-day occurrence that affect only the group of workers on whose behalf the shop steward is entitled to speak, he said:

Having brought such a matter to the management's attention the job steward's only further right is to notify his union should the grievance not be remedied. From that point the job steward necessarily drops out of the picture and the union officials take charge. Major matters of dispute affecting all the workers concerned or the majority of workers in a particular union should from the very beginning be handled by the Union. The job steward's only authority is to report the matter to the union which will then determine what should be done . . . We have heard too often the excuse that shop stewards, being elected by the workers, must do as the workers they represent direct. Such a statement is only partly true.[18] The only authority of the shop steward derives from the award and from the union rules. No direction from the men can authorize their taking action which is illegal, because contrary to the *Industrial Arbitration Act* or the award, or to the rules of the union of which they are members. I therefore suggest to the unions, parties to this award, that unless they wish to risk deregistration or other penalties because of the unauthorized action of shop stewards they give to every accredited shop steward a copy of the award and make it quite clear to him that he, as a worker and as the accredited representative of other workers, members of the union, is in duty bound to observe the provisions of the award and the rules of the union, and will be held personally responsible by both the Court and the Union for any non-observance of those provisions.[19] Such shop stewards must also be made to realize, and I believe union officials are the best persons to make it clear to them, that any breaches

---

[18] 'It is', the Full Bench of the Industrial Commission of New South Wales said, a 'complete misconception of the position, that a delegate is no more than a mouthpiece for the men whom he represents'—*In re Dispute at Broken Hill Pty Co. Ltd Steel Works, Newcastle (No. 2)* (1961) 60 A.R. (N.S.W.), at 67. See also pp. 17-18.

[19] A shop steward in an industrial union registered as such under the Industrial Arbitration Act, 1912-1963 of Western Australia, is in a position to make himself conversant, with little expense or inconvenience, with his powers and obligations under the rules of his union. Under section 23 of that Act he is entitled to obtain, from the secretary of the union, a printed copy of the rules for the time being of that union, on payment to him of a sum that is not to be in excess of one shilling. There is a similar provision under federal arbitration legislation. As a matter of fact, many of the Australian unions, particularly those registered under federal or New South Wales industrial law, supply copies of their rules to their members, free of charge. See O. de R. Foenander, *Trade Unionism in Australia*, pp. 130-1.

of the award or contraventions of the Act may well lead to the deregistration of the union . . . It therefore behoves a union to make the position quite clear to its shop stewards, particularly, as well as to its other members, and also to adopt as a matter of union policy the principle of withdrawing the accreditation of any shop steward who refuses to obey the Union rules and the resolutions or instructions of the properly elected Committee of Management of the Union. If those matters are properly understood I think the clause we propose inserting in the award should serve a useful purpose: if on the other hand we find that the job stewards in the future fail to observe the award and the union continues their accreditation, the union will have to take the responsibility for their actions,[20] and the court will also have to reconsider whether the award should embody any recognition at all of such job stewards as representing the workers concerned.[21]

It will be noticed that Mr Justice Nevile in criticizing and deprecating the view taken by some shop stewards of the nature of their function makes no practical suggestions, by way of an improvement, beyond recommending that union officials should provide their shop stewards with a copy of the award governing the industry in which they serve, and strongly impress on them the need for complying with the terms of the award and the rules of the union. He might, perhaps, have been expected to urge that some provision should be forthcoming to assist these persons to a true understanding of the meaning and implications of the award, and the rules that they are called upon to obey.[22] Perhaps, too, he might have found the occasion fitting—having regard to the wide programmes for the spread of education in all its phases in Australia, and the finance and other facilities made available to give effect to these developments[23]—to express an opinion as to the adequacy, or otherwise, of any schemes in operation in Australia at the present time or that are in prospect for the training of shop stewards, particularly in so far as they

---

20 In *In re Steel Works Employees (Broken Hill Proprietary Company Limited) and Iron and Steel Works Employees (Australian Iron and Steel Limited—Port Kembla) Awards (No. 1)* (1962), 61 A.R. (N.S.W.), at 362, the Full Bench of the New South Wales Industrial Commission said that it 'regards delegates or shop stewards as representatives of their union and regards unions as responsible for the actions of their delegates'.

21 *Western Australian Industrial Gazette*, vol. 43, no. 3 (1963), pp. 701-2.

22 It may be noted that some of the English trade unions issue, to their shop stewards, a credential card containing, *inter alia*, information and instructions as to the function and responsibilities of these stewards.

23 See p. 20.

have a relation to the powers and responsibilities attaching to the position, and the standards of conduct on the shop floor required from holders of the position.

Training of Shop Stewards in Great Britain

More recently the problem of the shop steward—certainly more acute in Great Britain than in Australia[24]—has stimulated interest afresh in that country, and in 1962 the British Minister of Labour suggested to the National Joint Advisory Council to the Minister of Labour (N.J.A.C.) that it should consider the question of the training of these persons. The suggestion was accepted by the N.J.A.C., and an initial examination made of proposals submitted to it by the Minister. The representatives of the Trades Union Congress General Council (T.U.C.G.C.) on the N.J.A.C. asserted, for their part, that it was

primarily the job of trade unions to provide training and that although they did not rule out the possibility of useful help from courses provided outside the trade union movement they were doubtful whether technical colleges or extra-mural departments were suitably staffed to give stewards practical training in their duties.[25]

The T.U.C.G.C., nevertheless, expressed its willingness to discuss with the British Employers' Confederation (B.E.C.) plans for the expansion of the training of shop stewards, on the basis that employers should allow shop stewards in their employment time off, without deduction of pay, to enable them to attend the appropriate courses of instruction. The B.E.C., in stating its preparedness to enter into discussions, said that if employers were to release shop stewards during working hours for the purpose, and pay their wages for the lost time, they would require to be consulted in regard to the form, and content, of the proposed courses.

Talks followed between representatives of the T.U.C.G.C. and the B.E.C., in a study of the subject along these lines, and as a result general accord was reached. The main points agreed upon were: (a) the need for an increased amount of systematic training of shop stewards, or their equivalent in function, so that a

[24] See pp. 24, 37-8.
[25] See *Report of 94th Annual Trades Union Congress, 1962* (published by authority of the Congress and General Council, 1962), p. 124.

greater number of this class of persons would be equipped with a broader and more adequate understanding of their province, and the responsibilities that it involves; (b) the desirability of more training, in working hours, as a means of achieving the hoped-for expansion of the training programme; and (c) an acknowledgment that the training was primarily the task of the trade unions, but that, when questions of facilities such as the allowance of time off without deduction of pay arise, the employers and the unions should reach some agreement before the constituents of the educational syllabus are decided upon for adoption. It was further agreed that, in reference to the purpose and content of training courses, no standard or common pattern was to be observed, but that, on the contrary, the courses should vary in accordance with the differing conditions prevailing in the different industries, the differing practices obtaining in the different trade unions, and the educational requirements of the individual steward as the occasion arises. Agreement, too, was arrived at in relation to certain details and aspects of the courses of instruction to be pursued, for (i) induction training (for example, the provision of a measure of background information relating to the structure, work and general policies of the union of the particular steward); (ii) basic training (e.g. the provision in appropriate cases of additional opportunities for stewards to acquire a wider knowledge of the organization of their union, and of its rules, practices and affairs); and (iii) practical training (e.g. the provision of instruction in arithmetical calculations involved in some of the more difficult, or abstruse, kinds or forms of wage payment, in the use of the English language both in speech and writing, and how to conduct workshop negotiations).[26]

Australian Trade Unionism and Trade Union Education

As yet, organized trade unionism in Australia has not made any substantial contribution to the solution of the problems of education as they have developed—in their particular relation to the trade unions, or otherwise. Little of what has actually been achieved by it in this respect has, as a matter of fact, been done at the national level. Such matters, in so far as they have been

26 See *Report of 95th Annual Trades Union Congress, 1963,* pp. 190-2.

the subject of practical treatment have, for the most part, been dealt with by the State Trades and Labour Councils, and through the Victorian Labor College and the individual trade unions (mainly by the courses that they have prepared and conducted for the training of officers and holders of positions in their organization). The A.C.T.U. Congress has spoken in broad terms of the need to inaugurate and support adequate educational schemes aimed at the protection and advancement of the various interests of the trade unions and the working population; it has declared that 'education in Trade Union objectives and Trade Union practices is essential'.[27] But up to the present it has stopped short, in this connection, at the enunciation of principles that in its opinion should be followed, and recommending that its Executive 'be authorized to set up a Committee to devise ways and means of furthering working class education in accordance with these principles'.[28] As will be seen, it certainly has not matched the effort of the British Trades Union Congress in planning, or taking action, to deal with the educational problems that, in many respects, are common to present-day industry in both Great Britain and Australia.

A body known as the Trade Union Education Committee has, however, been constituted in terms of the A.C.T.U. Congress recommendation, and is now engaged in collecting and examining additional information from all the States relative to existing facilities available for working-class education in Australia. No report of any kind of its investigations, or touching upon any phase of the subject, has yet been submitted for the consideration of Congress. Meantime, Congress itself has made no additional decisions on the question of trade union education, and it is believed that it will refrain from further action in this regard pending the presentation of a report from the Committee embodying the substance of the results of its inquiries. As will be gathered from what has already been said, Congress has not devoted any particular attention to the training of shop stewards, but it can be expected that this aspect of trade union education will come in for study by it when that body has before it the findings and conclusions of the Committee, or some of them.

[27] See *Decisions of the Australian Congress of Trade Unions, 4-8 September 1961,* issued by the A.C.T.U. (Melbourne, 1961), p. 14.
[28] Ibid. See also p. 88.

Supervisory Training for the Workshop in
Great Britain and Australia

A consideration of educational courses for shop stewards natu-
rally suggests a brief reference at least to what has been effected,
in this respect, with regard to those charged by management
with the duty of supervising operations in the workshop, for
example, foremen. There is a close industrial relationship between the holders of these positions, over and above that originating in their common employment. They correspond to each
other as opposites, so to speak, with parallel yet complementary
tasks and responsibilities to discharge. Just as the shop steward
is the representative of the trade union on the floor of the shop,
so the foreman is, in that place, the representative of the employer—as Mr Justice Higgins said of postmasters in the public
service in *The Commonwealth Postmasters' Association; Ex parte*
Australian Commonwealth Post and Telegraph Officers' Associ-
ation, he stands 'between the employer and other employees'.[29]
Efficiency in the supervisor is a factor in the betterment of
labour relations just as it is in the shop steward.[30] A standard in-
gredient in the content of educational schemes for supervisors
is, as in the case of shop stewards, *mutatis mutandis,* an understanding of the position of the shop steward and a knowledge
of the duties and responsibilities that attach to it.[31] Industrial
leaders are in general agreement that the initiative and greater
share in the training of candidates for supervisory posts are es-

[29] (1913) 7 C.A.R., at 57.
[30] 'There is an urgent need for more and better training of supervisors in
the interests of . . . improved relations between managements and their
employees'—*Report of the Committee on the Selection and Training of*
Supervisors (London, 1962), p. 32. The Committee was appointed by the
Minister of Labour (Great Britain), to 'review the progress made since the
publication in 1954 of the Report of the Committee of Inquiry on the Training of Supervisors, and the problems which have been encountered in organ-
izing effective training schemes, to consider arrangements for the selection
of supervisors and to examine whether there is a need for a central organization to further the development of supervisory training.' It is of note that
the Trades Union Congress was represented on the membership of the Committee. See also Carl Heyel, *Management for Modern Supervisors* (American
Management Association, 1962), pp. 71-3.
[31] Cf. *Report of the Committee on the Selection and Training of Super-*
visors, p. 15. Burleigh B. Gardner and David G. Moore, *Human Relations*
in Industry, p. 133, point out that, if a shop steward is to be 'effective', it
is essential that he appreciate the problems of the foreman as well as those
of the workers—'why the foreman does the things he does and what pres-
sures he is under'.

sentially, and for the most part, a matter for enterprise, in much the same way as they believe that the training of aspirants for the shop steward function is principally, and in the first instance, the concern or affair of the trade unions themselves.

It is difficult to state categorically and in positive terms whether in Australia, in reference to the workshop, more thought has been expended upon the preparation of men for management representation than has been afforded in relation to trade union representation. The author's opinion is that, in the field of supervisory training, Australia has not progressed to the same extent as Great Britain, in much the same way as it can be said that, in a comparison between the two countries regarding what has been achieved in the area of shop steward education, on the evidence available the advantage must be conceded as belonging to Great Britain. Up to the present there has not appeared in Australia any publication of the class of the British *Report of the Committee on the Selection and Training of Supervisors.* This is a valuable statement, concise and lucid in its expression, of the principles and problems of supervisory training for industry that must prove highly useful to students of labour relations, trade unionism and business administration everywhere.[32]

Allusion may here be made to the recognition extended by Australian industrial tribunals to the embarrassing position, arising out of their employment, in which foremen and supervisors can often be placed in relation to shop stewards and other operatives in the establishments over whose work they are called upon to exercise a measure of authority or control. These authorities realize that the loyalty of such persons to their employers may be jeopardized and the efficacy of their duties seriously affected as a consequence by a knowledge that discipli-

[32] The Minister of Labour has written in a foreword to the Report that it 'makes clear the shortcomings of the present arrangements in industry and suggests ways in which they can be improved.' It shows, he adds, that 'much more needs to be done by managements to ensure that their supervisors are trained and that the training given fits the supervisor for his particular job'. The Minister goes on to say that it recommends 'action by employers' associations, voluntary organizations, educational bodies and the Government to stimulate interest, provide advice and information to managements and develop training facilities', and, as he assesses the findings of the Committee responsible for its preparation, the Report 'gives practical guidance on the problems and difficulties of training'.

nary steps may be taken against them by executives of the
union, where shop stewards, or other fellow members of the
union, complain of their actions when directing or superintending
tasks in the course of employment. On that account, the industrial tribunals have been strongly inclined to favour applications,
on the part of bodies or associations constituted of employees
in charge of others, that seek independent registration as an
organization under the appropriate arbitration legislation. The
Commonwealth Court of Conciliation and Arbitration, for example, showed its appreciation of the difficult situation, in this
respect, in which senior officers of the Post and Telegraph Service of the Commonwealth sometimes found themselves. In up-
holding a claim for registration as an organization under the
Act, as it then stood, made by an association of officials described
as 'The Commonwealth Postmasters' Association'—apart from
that to which the operatives whom they supervised belonged—the
President of the Commonwealth Court of Conciliation and Arbitration, Mr Justice Higgins, remarked that one 'can easily con-
ceive of cases in which the duties of the postmasters might conflict with the interests of the general body of post office employees'.[33] The successful outcome of the proceeding, and the
combination of these persons in their own separate registered
organization, enabled them to attend to their responsibilities
to their superiors in the Commonwealth Public Service, and the
rest of the community, without the same fears that they had
entertained of being penalized by the union of which they were
members. They were equally assured that their industrial demands could be adequately and efficiently brought to the notice
and hearing of the Court, because the new registration entitled
a right of representation before the Court distinct from that by
the organization to which they previously belonged, and of
whose membership they comprised but a small minority exercising relatively little influence in the conduct of its affairs.

33 *The Commonwealth Postmasters' Association; Ex parte Australian Commonwealth Post and Telegraph Officers' Association* (1913) 7 C.A.R., at 57.
The Registrar of the Court, as an authority of first instance, had decided to
grant the application of the recently formed association of postmasters for
registration, and the matter had come before Mr Justice Higgins for review
by way of an appeal against the decision. See also O. de R. Foenander, *Wartime Labour Developments in Australia* (Melbourne, 1943), pp. 50-2, and his

Prevalence of Shop Stewards

In Australia, as in Great Britain and the United States, shop stewards or their equivalent in function under another name are to be found in a considerable number of unions,[34] but it is difficult to generalize as to the class of union in which they are located. As in the case of Great Britain, they are no longer confined to the craft unions.[35] It can be claimed with confidence, however, that they are more a feature of the larger organizations than of the smaller; nonetheless, in some of the important unions the rules make no provision for the post. They are not to any marked extent in the services occupations—'white collar' or otherwise; on the other hand, commodity-production industries can be cited in which no appointments have been made. The only explanation for their presence or absence, as the case may be, would appear to lie in the character of the particular industry or calling—the consideration of suitability or appropriateness of these persons to the conditions, or other factors calculated, in the circumstances, to enable them to serve a successful purpose.

Convenors

'Convenor' is an expression that does not loom largely in Australian industrial nomenclature, certainly not to the extent that it does in Great Britain and elsewhere. In truth not many of the Australian trade unions provide in their rules for the appointment of persons bearing that description. Of those that do the most important is the A.E.U., the rules of which, as a matter of fact, are portion of the rules of its parent union, the English Amalga-

---

Trade Unionism in Australia, pp. 41-2, where other of the cases as well are quoted or cited.

[34] In regard to Great Britain, Harry Welton, *The Trade Unions, the Employers and the State* (London, 1960), p. 116, believes that the 'majority of unions have representatives in the factories and workshops, where shop stewards, or others carrying out much the same functions under different names, recruit members'. But, according to H. A. Clegg *et al.*, *Trade Union Officers*, p. 29, 'many unions have no shop stewards'. The view of W. Milne-Bailey, expressed in 1929, would seem to incline more to that of Harry Welton than to that of H. A. Clegg *et al.* Mr Milne-Bailey, *Trade Union Documents* (London, 1929), p. 81, said: 'Most unions have their Collectors, Shop Stewards, Walking Delegates etc. (different names are used in different trades).'

[35] The shop steward system in general, as H. A. Turner, *Trade Union Growth, Structure and Policy*, p. 287, points out, has its beginnings in the old craft unions.

mated Engineering Union.[36] Under these rules it is the right of
the shop stewards, or the shop committee in a works or department, to elect a convenor of shop stewards who, it is required,
must himself be a shop steward. This person is authorized to
summon meetings of the shop stewards in the establishment, at
which matters may be discussed in implementation of policy
endorsed by the appropriate district committee of the union.
Among his obligations is the duty to inspect and sign, at quarterly intervals, the contribution cards of shop stewards in the
works or department in which his function is discharged. In the
carrying out of his duties he is responsible to the relative district
committee.

Women Appointees

As far as the writer is aware there is one Australian trade
union only whose rules make particular provision for the appointment of women shop stewards—the A.E.U. Under the rules of
this union women members of the union are enabled to be
stewards in shops where members of the women and girls section of the union are employed, but it is stipulated as a prerequisite for appointment that they shall be at least eighteen years of
age, and have been occupied in the engineering trade for a
period of not less than twelve months; where, however, this
temporal qualification requirement cannot be applied in a particular shop, the appropriate district committee of the union is
empowered to use its discretion to adjust the matter. These
stewards are elected by members of the section in the shop in
which they are employed, and their authority to represent is
restricted to the coverage of such members. Their rights, duties
and responsibilities are of the same nature as those that apply
to male shop stewards of the union, and they are subject to the
general rules of the union governing shop stewards. They are

---

36 According to the Rules of the Amalgamated Engineering Union the
Commonwealth Council of the Amalgamated Engineering Union (Australian
Section) is, as regards certain matters, under the direction and control of the
Executive Council of the Amalgamated Engineering Union. The Executive
Council is constituted of members of the Amalgamated Engineering Union,
and represents English branches only of the union; it is located in the United
Kingdom. See *Re Elections for Offices in Amalgamated Engineering Union
(Australian Section)* (1961) 3 F.L.R. 63; the decision of the Commonwealth
Industrial Court in *Parkes v. Horsburgh and Others* (1962) 3 F.L.R. 281;
and O. de R. Foenander, *Trade Unionism in Australia*, pp. 9-10.

enjoined to collaborate with other shop stewards belonging to the union in the discharge of their obligations. It may be added that Australian industrial tribunals have usually been prepared to accept a provision in the rules of a union, denying the enjoyment of full membership rights to a member during some probationary or other qualifying period, conditionally upon the specified period being capable of being regarded as not unreasonable in the circumstances.[37]

Although the rules of a union, unlike those of the A.E.U., may not specifically provide for women shop stewards, objection cannot be taken to their introduction if the rules permit of the appointment of shop stewards, unless there is an express or implied discrimination in the rules against women acting in this capacity. Women, as a matter of fact, fulfil the usual duties of shop stewards in a multiplicity of industries and callings, especially those where female workers predominate in number or are in force—for example, in the clothing trades (where, under the Rules of the Clothing and Allied Trades Union of Australia express provision is made for the appointment of shop stewards without any mention of women), and in the food preserving industry (where, under the Rules of the Food Preservers' Union of Australia, no express provision is made for the appointment of shop stewards at all, leaving it open to a presumption that the power to appoint shop stewards of either sex is implied in the rules).

The presence of women shop stewards has proved of decided advantage in divisions of the factory where females are employed, notably in regard to the matter of amenities of various kinds, and it seems to be generally agreed that little friction or disharmony has arisen between male and female shop stewards where they perform their duties in the same establishment.

'Sick' Stewards

There is a provision in the Rules of the A.E.U.—not found, as far as the author is aware, in the rules of any other Australian union—to the effect that where one of its members meets with an accident, industrial or otherwise, or is the victim of a mental

[37] Cf. judgments of the Court in *Cameron* v. *Australian Workers' Union* (1959) 2 F.L.R. 45; and *MacDonald* v. *Amalgamated Engineering Union* (*Australian Section*) (1962) 3 F.L.R. 446, particularly at 449 (per Joske J.).

derangement, and is incapable of presenting a claim for sick benefit to the appropriate branch of the union, 'sick' stewards shall visit him within twenty-four hours of receiving this information. The stewards, moreover, are obliged to make their visit without delay where the circumstances are such that the member's health is endangered, and they have knowledge of this fact. It is further incumbent on them to give immediate notice of the condition of the afflicted member to his relatives or friends. The stewards are entitled to payment on account of 'reasonable expenses' incurred by them in the performance of these duties. They can be described as members of the union who have been nominated to undertake, on a part-time basis, duties of a special kind. Their function is quite apart from that of the shop stewards, with whom they should not be confused.

The Plumbers and Gasfitters Employees' Union of Australia deals with the problem of rendering aid to members who are in difficulties—through illness or otherwise—without provision in its rules for any distinct or regular class of persons for this purpose. Its rules stipulate that where a member of the union is sick, or becomes 'unfinancial', a fellow member residing in the vicinity of his home may be appointed to call on this member and report upon the matter at the next meeting of the relevant branch, or committee of management of the branch. Where, at this meeting, an entitlement to an allowance or monetary assistance in some other form is established, an amount may be handed to the visiting member for payment, within forty-eight hours, to the person in favour of whom the sum was made available.

Claims for Preferential Treatment

From time to time demands have been made on behalf of shop stewards—mainly on the ground that a measure of independence is indispensable to them if they are to exercise their function without fear of intimidation or victimization from employers—the granting of which would place them in a situation of priority or privilege *vis-à-vis* their fellow workers. A good example is the claim for seniority rights, in terms of which when hands are shortened in conditions of business recession their lay-off would be postponed until all others of the classification in which they are engaged in the establishment have been stood

down, or have received notice of dismissal, and when trade
recovers, restoration to their jobs, if sought, would be effected
before any other of their classification has been re-employed.
These claims have usually been supported by the unions themselves.

No such favoured treatment of this, or a similar, kind is accorded to shop stewards under the provisions of Australian industrial legislation. In this respect the position in Australia is
not the same as that in some other countries, for example,
France, where in terms of the statutory law it is provided that
a shop steward may not be dismissed from his employment
unless the approval of the works committee in the establishment
(*comité d'entreprise*), or appropriate Inspector of Labour, is first
obtained. Other members of an Australian trade union share
with the shop steward the protection granted by section 5 of the
Act against dismissal or threats of dismissal, or injury or prejudice
in their employment or threats of injury or prejudice in their
employment, by reason of certain classes of industrial action on
their part.[38] Seniority claims in relation to the shop steward function have, however, been before the industrial tribunals, but
the decisions have usually shown a determination to uphold the
traditional right of management to freedom in the selection and
retention of employees. Thus, in one of the *Engine Drivers' and
Firemen's Cases,* O'Mara J. observed:

Included in claim dealing with shop stewards is one that in the
event of retrenchment of employees the shop steward shall be the
last employee of the classification in which he is engaged to be dismissed and if dismissed and employees are subsequently engaged he
shall if available be the first man to be re-engaged. I propose to discuss
this claim, not that it ever impressed me as having any merits but
so that my views on claims of this nature will be known. Such a
claim may possibly be justified on the ground that it is necessary to
give the shop steward sufficient independence in the carrying out
of his duties as the spokesman and representative of employees. To
interfere with an employer's right of management and selection of

[38] Similar provision is made by State industrial legislation; see section 95
of the Industrial Arbitration Act, 1940-1964 (New South Wales); section
101 of the Industrial Conciliation and Arbitration Acts, 1961-1963 (Queensland); section 122 of the Industrial Code, 1920-1963 (South Australia); and
section 135 of the Industrial Arbitration Act, 1912-1963 (Western Australia).
There is no industrial arbitration legislation in force in the other States; see
p. 13. See also pp. 88-90.

employees to the detriment of other and possibly better workmen
would be a very serious thing, and I can see no justification whatever
for such a serious curtailment of the rights of the employer and other
employees.[39]

In a *Ship Painters' and Dockers' Case* Mr Commissioner Tonkin,
in exercise of the jurisdiction of the Commission, concurred in
the substance of the remarks of the learned judge, and refused
the request of the union involved for the reinstatement of a
union delegate who had been dismissed as a consequence of
the slack conditions in the industry, in spite of the assertion,
strongly voiced by the union, that the employer company had
by its action disregarded the custom and practice existent over
many years in the industry governing the employment of delegates. The union, it may be added, had intimated that it was
willing that another man should be put off in order to maintain
the delegate in his post.[40] The Commissioner said:

To agree to the Union's proposal, which is to establish the greatest
degree of permanency of employment possible for its delegates,
would place such delegates in the position of being almost immune
from dismissal. This, I consider, would be a dangerous principle to
establish, as it would give them a power, by reason of their sense of
security in employment, which, in my opinion, delegates should not
possess. Such power would enable them to extend their scope far
beyond what are the recognized duties of delegates, and which are
contained in many awards. I feel it would create a dangerous precedent, if such power was indirectly given by this Commission to
delegates, as it could be used in such a way as to interfere with the
smooth working arrangements of the management.[41]

It may be mentioned, in passing, that careful note has usually
been taken by Australian industrial tribunals of a submission
based on custom or practice general to the industry, such as was
made in this case, provided the custom or practice is shown to
be well established or of long standing, is not inconsistent with
the provisions of an award or the rules of a union that is a party
to the proceedings, and is not in contravention of principles or
practices followed by the tribunal that is hearing the matter.

[39] *Federated Engine Drivers' and Firemen's Association of Australasia* v.
Adelaide Brick Co. Ltd and Others (1940) 42 C.A.R., at 612.
[40] *Morts Dock and Engineering Co. Ltd* v. *Federated Ship Painters' and
Dockers' Union of Australia* (1957) 88 C.A.R. 212.
[41] Ibid., at 213. See also pp. 69-70.

Little attempt, however, has been made by the courts to clarify the meaning of—much less to define—the expressions 'custom' and 'practice' as they appear in the context of such an argument.[42]

What, however, has been refused by industrial tribunals to shop stewards, in regard to preference in employment over fellow-workers in the shop, is being enjoyed by them in a number of industries by virtue of tacit understandings between employers and unions that have grown up over a number of years, and these have come to be looked upon as in the nature of a custom or established practice. A situation has thus developed which is similar, to an extent, to that existing in Great Britain and the United States where under the terms of many collective agreements shop stewards are placed at the top of the respective seniority lists of the plants and departments in point of disemployment and re-employment. Florence Peterson believes that such a provision 'serves as an inducement to assume the responsibilities of a stewardship, removes fear of discriminatory dismissal because of action taken in connection with the work of a steward, and safeguards continuity in grievance adjustment personnel'.[43]

Industrial Award Rights

In another direction, too, rights are available to shop stewards and they are calculated to assist them in the effective discharge of their duties—in this instance, under grant in some of the awards of the industrial tribunals themselves. These concessions are not at the expense, or to the detriment, of fellow workers, and since they do not involve any serious dislocation of entre-

[42] Among the principles observed by the industrial tribunals in their practice is a recognition of the dictates of public policy, and a full regard for the requirements of industrial efficiency and the conditions of the national progress. Thus Mr Conciliation Commissioner Buckland, an official operating under the dichotomous scheme of federal industrial regulation in force before the creation of the Commission and the Court in 1956 said, in giving his decision in the *Footwear Manufacturing Industry Award Case* (1953) 76 C.A.R., at 519-20: 'I feel that whilst customs of long standing in an industry are of great importance and must be given the necessary attention and consideration they must not be allowed both in the interests of the employer and the employee to effectively stand in the way and become a bar to progress and efficiency in an industry and this particularly so when the changes contemplated do not in any way adversely affect the interests of those concerned.'

[43] *American Labor Unions*, p. 163. In the view of H. A. Clegg *et al.*, *Trade Union Officers*, pp. 175-6, there is evidence of the existence of victimization of shop stewards in Great Britain at the hands of employers.

preneurial policy or disturb the conduct of operations in the
factory, they are not in any real sense to the prejudice of
management. The provision, where it appears, is usually in a
more or less standardized form, and extends to a diversity of
industries, jobs and callings. Clause 23 of the Transport Workers
(Airways) Award now in force is typical:

> An employee appointed shop steward in the depot or department in
> which he is employed shall, upon notification thereof to his employer
> by the Secretary of the Union, be recognized as the accredited repre-
> sentative of the Union to which he belongs, and he shall be allowed
> the necessary time during working hours to interview the employer
> or his representative on matters affecting employees whom he rep-
> resents.[44]

The corresponding clause (28) in the current Slaughtering,
Freezing and Processing Works (Meat Industry) Award supplies
an example of a departure, in substance, from this norm. It provides for the appointment, from time to time, of two representatives of the union[45] in each works in which the award applies, for
an obligation on the part of the employer to recognize them as
such on notification to that effect in writing, and for the right of
these representatives to interview the appropriate representative of
the employer at a reasonable time on matters affecting members
of the union employed at such works; such representatives must
be employees in the works concerned. But the clause further
stipulates that a works representative is not authorized to leave
his work in exercise of this right to interview without the permission of the foreman or other person for the time being in
charge of his department, the permission, however, not to be
'unreasonably' refused if an 'urgent' matter should arise for consideration. Furthermore, this representative is not entitled to
payment during his absence from work, unless the absence is at
the request of the employer.[46] The relevant provision in the

---

[44] Shorter in length and simpler in expression, clause 25 of the Glass
Workers' Award provides that a 'shop steward shall be permitted for and on
behalf of the employees, and he shall be empowered to approach the employer at any time on their behalf'.

[45] The union here mentioned is the Australasian Meat Industry Employees'
Union.

[46] In regard to a provision in a State award similar to that contained in this
clause, see clause 17 of the Metal Trades Construction (Alumina Refinery)
Award, 1962 (Western Australia)—*Western Australian Government Gazette*,
no. 99 (7 December 1962). For examples of slight variations from what may

current Engine Drivers' and Firemen's (State Electricity Commission of Victoria) Award, contained in clause 23, adds that the provision is not to apply at any place where five or less persons are employed.

A provision of this character in an award must be distinguished from another, and more usual, clause in an award in accordance with which an accredited representative of a union is conceded the right to enter an employer's premises where work is being carried on under the award for the purpose, *inter alia,* of interviewing individual employees on legitimate union business and investigating complaints concerning the application of the award. Indeed, in certain awards now operative, both of these matters are covered, that is, the right of the shop steward to interview the employer or his representative, and the right of an authorized union official to enter the establishment to interview union employees, etc. Examples are the current Transport Workers (Airways) Award, Northern Territory (Oil Companies) Award, Clothing Trades Award, Gas Industry Award, Metal Trades Award, Carpenters and Joiners Award, Manufacturing Grocers Award, Glass Workers Award and Shipwrights (Shore) Award.

Australian industrial tribunals, on a number of occasions, have commented on the significance of these award entitlements of shop stewards and union delegates to discuss with management grievances originating in employment in the workshops, and they have been careful to insist on the observance of the terms on which the privilege has been granted, and referred to the obligations to which it gives rise. Thus the Full Bench of the Industrial Commission of New South Wales said, in *In re dispute at Broken Hill Pty Co. Ltd Steelworks, Newcastle (No. 2):* 'The right to recognition and to be allowed time to interview the

---

be described as the standard form of the provision, see clause 41 of the current Carpenters and Joiners Award, and clause 41 of the current Builders Labourers (Construction on Site) Award. Clause 52 of the Graphic Arts (Interim) Award, 1957, as amended to and including 8 July 1963, provides for the rate at which a union delegate, employed as a piece-worker in an employment covered by the award, shall be paid for time spent by him in interviewing the employer. The clause runs as follows: 'Not more than two delegates, chosen by and from the employees of an employer, shall be allowed the necessary time in working hours to interview the employer or his representative for the purpose of submitting grievances. If the delegate or delegates so chosen be piece workers they shall be paid for such time the time worker's wage in their branch of industry.'

company or its representative in working hours is a valuable one, but it carries with it corresponding responsibilities.'[47]

An interesting observation was made by the President of the Industrial Commission of New South Wales (Taylor J.), when giving a decision in 1956 in reference to a dispute at St Mary's Project, 590 (New South Wales), on the expression, 'union business', in its relation to the function of a job representative. The dispute had arisen out of the dismissal of a number of operatives from their employment, twelve of whom were job representatives of various industrial unions. The men had been discharged on the ground that they had held an unauthorized meeting in the course of working hours in a shed on the premises of the employer company. They claimed that the meeting was for the purpose of attending to union business.

It was shown to the satisfaction of the President that the company had approved of the principle that a union representative should be accorded leave from his work, on occasions, to attend to union business conditionally, *inter alia*, upon permission to do so having been first obtained from officials of the company. The company denied that approval had been granted by it for the holding of the meeting, or that it had been, in fact, sought, and this assertion was accepted and upheld by the President.

The learned President found that the job representatives had been dismissed with just cause, and accordingly confirmed the action of the company in terminating their employment.[48] He said that union business

as I see it . . . in the concept generally understood is the doing of something by a Union representative in respect of a particular matter raised by a member of his Union. This particular matter would need to be raised before some person in a position of authority with the Company who could resolve the trouble. A gathering of a large number of Union representatives, with only Union representatives in attendance, without reference to the Company's officials, is in quite a different category.[49]

47 (1961) 60 A.R. (N.S.W.), at 66-7.
48 The case is not reported in either the New South Wales Arbitration Reports, or the *New South Wales Industrial Gazette*. The only authoritative record of the findings of the President is as set out in the official Transcript of Proceedings of the Industrial Commission of New South Wales, June 1956, vol. 325.   49 Ibid., pp. 717C, 717D.

Political Electoral Activity

The most recent general election for seats in the House of Representatives—the Lower House of the federal legislature— provided an example of more than usual interest, in one way at least, of the close co-operation that has always been a feature of the relations between the political and industrial wings of the labour movement in Australia;[50] for the first time, the services of trade union officers and shop stewards were systematically availed of in the organization of the collaboration. The arrangement was the outcome of a meeting, convened during the electoral campaign by the Melbourne Trades Hall Council of trade union officers and shop stewards, with the object of stimulating and intensifying 'on the job' canvassing activity directed to the return of A.L.P. candidates at the polls. It is recognized that such persons have special opportunities for putting the argument for the A.L.P. before workers in the factories and on the sites, by explaining in a simple, straight-forward and informal manner the various items in the party's programme, answering questions in relation to them, and replying to allegations and criticisms touching the issues involved that had been levelled by political opponents, etc. This can be said to apply more particularly in the case of shop stewards, mainly because of the facilities that they daily enjoy for access to, or contact with, fellow operatives on the work benches, or for approaches to them during the lunch hour, or at 'smoke-oh' time, or during morning and afternoon tea breaks. It is worthy of note, too, that union officers and shop stewards who were present at the meeting were compensated for the loss of wages, incurred by them as the result of their attendance, out of contributions by trade unionists to a collection taken up among themselves for that purpose.

The Shop Steward and Official Machinery for the Settlement of Industrial Disputes

Recent developments in award-making by the Australian industrial tribunals show an increasing recognition of the usefulness of the shop stewardship or union delegateship as a factor

50 See O. de R. Foenander, *Trade Unionism in Australia*, pp. 22-3.

in the maintenance of the industrial peace. Provisions have been inserted in awards that may be said to incorporate this position as a definite part in the authoritative machinery for the settlement of disputes in industry, and the ensuring of continuity in industrial operations. Reference can be made, in this connection, to clause 30 of the Transport Workers (Passenger Coaches) Award, as varied, and clause 6 of the Aluminium Industry Award (so far as it is concerned with the settlement of disputes). Both of these awards, including the variation, were made by the Commission in the course of the year 1963, and they are specifically declared to be subject to the Act. Clause 18 of the Metal Trades Construction (Alumina Refinery) Award, promulgated by the Court of Arbitration of Western Australia in 1962 and dealing with the remedying of industrial grievances and the settlement of industrial disputes, is drawn on the same broad lines; some consideration has already been afforded to this clause in another context, namely, to illustrate the distinction in character and status between an office in a registered industrial union and the position of shop steward or job delegate in that organization.[51] The provisions in the federal awards alluded to vary because of, *inter alia,* the differing natures of, and practices in, the industries to which they relate, and the differing constitutional structures of, and procedures in, the trade unions that are parties to the award in question. But while the divergences in the provisions are not great, they are sufficiently substantive, in the author's opinion, to warrant setting out the relevant material contents of the clause in each case.

In the first of these awards of the Commission, it is stipulated that any matter in dispute that is not referred by the parties to the Board of Reference, in pursuance of clause 28 of the award, shall be the subject of negotiations to be conducted in accordance with the procedure ordinarily observed by the parties, or in the manner prescribed as follows:

(1) The matter is to be taken up by the union delegate with the branch manager or other appropriate officer of the employer concerned, or by this manager or officer with the delegate, as the case may be.

---

[51] See *Western Australian Government Gazette,* no. 99 (7 December 1962); see also p. 16.

(2) Should no agreement be arrived at as the result of these conversations, the matter is to be taken up by the branch secretary of the union with the employer, or by the employer with this secretary, as the case may be.

(3) In the event of a settlement being still not reached, the matter is to be discussed between the principal offices of the employer and the union.

(4) Should the parties fail in their efforts at agreement by observing either their ordinary procedure, or by following the sequence of steps prescribed in the award, the matter must be referred by them to a member of the Commission for decision. But a proviso is appended to the effect that, in any 'case of urgency', the course of negotiations as thus outlined may be shortened by the omission of one, or more, of the stages preceding the reference to a member of the Commission. No attempt is made by the award to define the words, 'case of urgency', or otherwise indicate their meaning, for purposes of the clause and the award.

The award with respect to the aluminium industry provides that, except as stipulated in clause 27,[52] any dispute or claim arising out of the operation of the award is to be dealt with in accordance with the following procedure:

(1) Submission of the matter by the shop steward or union representative to the industrial officer, or other appropriate officer, of the employer concerned.

(2) Failing a settlement by this method, formal submission of the matter by the State secretary or other appropriate official of the union concerned to the employer concerned.

(3) If there is still no agreement, the matter to be discussed between the head office of the employer concerned and the federal body of the union concerned.

(4) Should the matter remain not settled in spite of these attempts, a submission of the matter to the Commission for decision.

It is further provided that, while this procedure is being observed, work shall continue normally where it is agreed that

---

[52] This clause provides for an entitlement of employees on weekly hiring to sick leave without deduction of pay, and for the conditions and limitations governing that entitlement.

there is an existing custom, but that in other cases it must go on at the instruction of the employer concerned, unless danger is involved; in the latter case the work is not to proceed pending a decision on the matter. No party, however, is to be prejudiced with regard to the final settlement by a continuance of work in terms of this provision.

Some notable absences from the second award of provisions that appear in the first award will be noticed; for example, there is no alternative course of action that would permit a resort to a usual procedure, established by the parties themselves for the settlement of disputes, and no opportunity for direct reference to the Commission, in circumstances of emergency, where the prescribed antecedent procedure has not been fully obeyed. On the other hand, in the first award there is no provision for, and governing, a continuance of work while the prescribed procedure is being operated. From the evidence available it would appear that the unions are not in agreement with the imposition of a ban on the discontinuance of work in the form that it assumes in clause 6 of the Aluminium Industry Award. However, the qualification of this requirement in the interests of the safety of employees whose employment is regulated by the award should serve to deprive their objections and criticisms of much of their force.

A few weeks before the Transport Workers (Passenger Coaches) Award was varied to add clause 30 to it, another award —known as the 'Transport Workers (Pioneer Tourist Coaches) Prohibition of Bans, Limitations and Restrictions Award, 1963' —had been issued. The title of the award denotes its object and substance—namely, to forbid any organization that is party to the award to be in any way, whether directly or indirectly, a party to or concerned in any ban, limitation or restriction with respect to work performed, or to be performed, in accordance with the Transport Workers (Pioneer Tourist Coaches) Agreement, 1957.[53]

Such a provision in an award is commonly called the 'anti-bans clause', or more simply, the 'bans clause'. Contravention or disregard of its terms invites the imposition of a penalty by the

[53] This agreement was superseded by the Transport Workers (Passenger Coaches) Award, 1963, just referred to.

Court through the machinery of sections 109 and 111 of the Act. A party proved to the satisfaction of the Court to have broken or not observed the clause may, under section 109, be enjoined by it from continuing the infringement or non-observance, as the case may be, and a failure to comply with the order renders the offending organization liable, under section 111, to a penalty for a contempt of its power and authority.[54] The anti-bans clause has been introduced into a number of awards, and the sanctions that can follow its infringement or disregard, by the conjunctive application of the sections, are available also as a protection to such provisions as are contained in clause 30 of the Transport Workers (Passenger Coaches) Award, and clause 6 of the Aluminium Industry Award, against breach or non-observance.

The inclusion of clause 30 in the first-named of these awards might seem to make superfluous, and therefore unnecessary, the existence or operation of the Transport Workers (Pioneer Tourist Coaches) Prohibition of Bans, Limitations and Restrictions Award; to say the least, its presence robs the award of something of its significance.[55] At any rate the latter award was declared to be rescinded by Mr Gough, of the Commission, by the same order that amended the Transport Workers (Passenger Coaches) Award to add clause 30. The Commissioner took the view that the retention of the award was not logically justified, so that the repeal can be regarded as in the nature of a consequential step.[56]

Assessment of New Provisions in Awards for Settling Industrial Disputes

Opinions of the virtues and shortcomings of the new process prescribed in awards and designed as a safeguard for industry against the occurrence of strikes and work stoppages vary, almost of necessity. Much depends on the point of view, the nature of,

[54] For some critical remarks on the operation of these sections, see the dissenting judgment of Kirby J. in *Australian Gas Light Co. and Another* v. *Federated Gas Employees' Industrial Union* (1950) 68 C.A.R., at 455-65. Under the ruling of the High Court in *Seamen's Union of Australasia* v. *Commonwealth Steamship Owners' Association and Others* (1935-6) 54 C.L.R. 626, the Commission has authority to incorporate an anti-bans clause in its awards. See also pp. 93-5.

[55] As to the desirability of adopting both provisions for purposes of one award, see the remarks on p. 81.　　[56] See p. 74.

or the presence of some special feature or features in, the industry concerned and the interests to be served. Undeniably there is much in it to recommend, representing as it may be said to do a *via media* between a method in accordance with which severe penalties for breaches or non-observances of awards, particularly those containing the anti-bans clause, can readily be imposed, and a condition where there is a complete absence of any stipulation for punishment for actions and failures in these respects. The scheme could thus be expected to appeal to those who, while deploring what they consider to be the harshness of the incidence that is possible by the conjunctive operation of the Act and awards incorporating the anti-bans clause, realize that at some stage when the parties to an award are in dispute authoritative intervention and legal sanctions in some form or measure must be available if compulsory arbitration is to have any real meaning at all, and the efficacy of the present system of federal industrial regulation is to be preserved. To Mr Winter, of the Commission, clause 25 of the Engineering (Oil Companies) Award, 1958, which is in terms similar to those of that part of clause 6 of the Aluminium Industry Award, 1963, that deals with the settlement of disputes, 'seems . . . to be an ideal type of clause, providing an orderly and logical type of approach to settlement of a dispute'.[57]

When it comes to the matter of an uninhibited preference between the newer and older provisions, very probably employers are attracted, or at least incline, to the anti-bans clause, because in the event of its breach or non-observance a direct application can be made to the Court without more ado, if they so desire, for an injunctive order under section 109 of the Act, which, if not obeyed, could be followed by a punishment of the guilty party in furtherance of section 111.[58] In this way the delay entailed in the holding of the successive discussions and consultations between disputants or their representatives and the reference of the matter to the Commission in the event of their

[57] See *In the matter of Engineering (Oil Companies) Award, 1958 (application by Standard-Vacuum Refining Co. (Australia) Pty Ltd to vary the award by the insertion of a bans clause)*, Transcript of Proceedings, 23 October 1963, p. 42. Seven large federal organizations of employees and eleven important companies engaged in the oil and oil-refining industries are parties to this award.
[58] See pp. 74-5.

failure, as required in terms of the new method, would be avoided and a more expeditious decision obtained by a trial of the issue in accordance with traditional legalistic practice, and with heavy reliance on an examination of documentary evidence.

It should be understood, however, that applications under section 109 are 'not mere routine', and that orders in pursuance of its provisions are not made as a matter of course. While the Court is under a duty to ensure to the best of its ability that awards will be observed, it is not obliged, nor is it prepared, to grant an order in terms of the section in the absence of 'ample justification'. In applying the section it has a responsibility to protect the interests of all concerned, and these interests are not confined to those of the parties to the award in question. The provisions of the section are for the benefit of the general public as well as for the benefit of the parties to the proceeding on which the award is based—the community has a 'vested interest' in the preservation of peace in all industrial operations.[59] As a matter of fact the number of applications seeking the injunctive order, including those brought under old section 29 of the Act, in the disposal of which an order for the desired injunction did not issue, does not fall short to any great extent of the number of those in connection with which the grant was duly made; according to official information 387 applications were filed to the end of August 1964, and in only 214 of these did the orders *nisi* succeed in being made absolute. Section 109 was inserted in the Act in supersession of section 29 under the authority of amending legislation passed in 1956.

On the other hand, strongly opposed as the unions are in practically any circumstances to the application of machinery by which penalties affecting themselves, or their members, can be imposed as the result of non-compliance with the provisions of awards, if an election has to be made they would presumably favour the newer procedure as the lesser of two evils, in that it provides, in the normal case, for a series of meetings at various levels between the parties in dispute or their spokesmen, and subsequent intervention by the Commission where differences

[59] See the judgment of Dunphy J. in *Commonwealth Steamship Owners' Association* v. *Waterside Workers' Federation of Australia* (1960), not reported in F.L.R. But see Print no. A7812 (Industrial Registrar), pp. 3-4.

have not been amicably adjusted by these means. There are thus various interpositions before peremptory action by the Court is to be anticipated. They do not forget, either, that if the matter in dispute passes beyond the phases of private negotiation to reach the stage of authoritative regulation, the Commission, by virtue of section 40(1) of the Act, is under a duty to proceed in the hearing and determination of the dispute according to 'equity, good conscience and the substantial merits of the case, without regard to technicalities and legal forms'. In addition, under the terms of the sub-section it is not bound to act in a formal manner, and there is no obligation on it to abide by or observe any rules of evidence; it is fully at liberty in the conduct of its hearings and the determination of issues involved to inform itself on any matter before it in such manner as to it appears just. Generous opportunities are thus open to the Commission for the cognizance and ascertainment of facts in its own way, and for flexibility in the application of such facts to the situation, enabling it to temper or alleviate, in its treatment of matters, the rigours of a strictly legal proceeding. There are no provisions of this nature in the Act affecting the practice of the Court, which is a legal authority purely and simply, invested with part of the judicial power of the Commonwealth. In contradistinction, the Commission is a conciliative and arbitral tribunal (with a responsibility for the performance of certain relatively minor tasks of an administrative character as well), and is not constitutionally a court of law.[60] Incidentally, the new procedure for the settlement of industrial disputes illustrates the true place of compulsory arbitration in the Australian theory and conception of labour regulation—namely, a reserve technique to be used only after all attempts by the parties themselves to come to an amicable agreement on the issue, or issues, involved have been exhausted.

There are signs that employers, in the face of the bitter objection of the unions to the presence of the anti-bans clause in awards, would be prepared to refrain in some circumstances from seeking its insertion and to acquiesce in the inclusion of the principle of the new provision in its stead. The explanation

---

[60] Cf. the decision of the High Court in *The Queen* v. *Kirby and Others; Ex parte Boilermakers' Society of Australia* (1956) 94 C.L.R. 254.

lies mainly in the interest that they have in the maintenance of the industrial peace. Apart from the pressure exerted by unions they may be moved, too, by the calculation that through the exploitation of the new method with efficiency and expedition strikes and work stoppages fomented by multi-union shop committees, and other unruly bodies of their kind, are less likely to arise. Under the newer awards, it will be remembered, shop stewards or their equivalent are bound to take up claims in dispute with the appropriate representatives of the employer concerned, and if agreement is not reached by them in conference the matter has then to be discussed by officers of the union and management at a higher level.

The A.C.T.U. has been seriously embarrassed, in recent days, by the tactics of multi-union shop committees and area committees in inducing stoppages in workshops where a dispute has arisen in regard to an industrial matter, before control of the dispute can be, or has been, assumed by the relevant union and union machinery is set in motion to deal with the situation. Describing developments such as these as amounting to a condition of 'industrial anarchy', Mr Commissioner Winter lamented that it was 'saddening to see the efforts of trade unions which are actively struggling in the interests of their members being aborted by the action of irresponsible and inflammatory members'.[61] When ordering the inclusion of an anti-bans clause in the Engineering (Oil Companies) Award, 1958, as sought, he disclosed that, mindful that 'ultimate responsibility for achieving industrial discipline of members rests with the trade unions',[62] he was pursuing this course in the hope that the organizations affected would be stirred to take command of what, as he believed, had evolved into a dangerous state of affairs. To him it was the 'very antithesis' of trade unionism where members were not willing to accept the decisions of those whom they had elected to become their leaders.[63] The instant intervention of the shop steward in a dispute, in terms of his obligation under the newer provision for the settlement of industrial disputes, should, in the author's opinion, prove highly useful in the reservation to

[61] See *In the matter of Engineering (Oil Companies) Award, 1958 (application by Standard-Vacuum Refining Co. (Australia) Pty Ltd to vary the award by the insertion of a bans clause)*, Transcript of Proceedings, 23 October 1963, p. 49.   [62] Ibid.   [63] Ibid., p. 42.

the union of effective control over matters that are properly its concern.

The new method, however, is at present scarcely beyond the tentative and experimental stage. Its future place in the codes of Australian industrial regulation must await, to a great extent, decisions as to whether the anti-bans clause is to remain in awards governing the group of industries known collectively as the metal trades, and other important industries. The current Metal Trades Award[64] was made in January 1952, and it was to continue in operation, as specified in its own terms, for a period of one year as on and from the beginning of the first pay period commencing in February of that year. Since the expiration of the period for which it was thus to last, it has been kept in force, as amended, by the operation of section 58(2) of the Act.[65] The extent of the prolongation of the life of this award authorized under the terms of the sub-section is, as will be observed, already considerable; the award has, however, been varied on many occasions. Those primarily interested in it, or responsible for its administration, would seem to agree that the method of altering it accordingly, from time to time, where it is decided to allow a change in a particular provision or provisions—involving a postponement of a revision *in toto* of the award pending the emergence of circumstances that make a thorough overhaul desirable —has given satisfaction; in the case of this award the expense and labour incidental to a complete review and necessary recasting would be considerable.

The metal trades unions are now seeking a further variation of the relative awards, aimed at the dropping of the anti-bans clause from them. It may be suggested that a determination concerning the withdrawal of the clause from any of the awards in question, or its reshaping, will depend largely on whether the Commission is persuaded that there has been an improvement in the industrial behaviour that led to its insertion, and whether it can be convinced that a continued improvement in this respect

[64] The award covers the engineering, metal-working and fabricating industries in all their branches, and all industries allied thereto. It is the principal award in connection with employment in the metal trades.

[65] The sub-section provides that, after the expiration of the term specified in the award for its duration, the award is to continue in force, unless the Commission otherwise orders, until a new award is made.

is likely. Or perhaps that authority may be content with assurances and undertakings that, for an approved period, the industrial peace will not be broken by the respective unions. If it allows the removal, it seems at least probable that it will order the introduction of a settlement of disputes provision in replacement. An interesting side-effect of the adoption of the course—deletion of the clause with the substitution of the provision—should be a gratification for those who feel that the Commission should exercise the fullest control over its own awards that is legally and constitutionally possible.

In the author's opinion there is much to be said against the writing of a settlement of disputes provision into awards regulating industries in which large numbers of employers and employees are engaged. Possibly a provision of this type is truly operable only where conditions are such that personal contact between employers and employees is usually reasonably close, and a measure of good feeling between labour and management normally prevails.

It may indeed be found feasible, in certain circumstances, to make a place for a settlement of disputes provision and the anti-bans clause within the confines of a single award, on the basis of a division of the matters to which the provision and the clause, respectively, are to apply. Insertions in accordance with this principle, carefully devised and appropriately arranged, should have something to contribute to the solution of the industrial problem.

The author believes that there is a future for the provision, and ventures to say that its inclusion in an increasing number of awards is to be anticipated. But he is hesitant, having in mind the industrial outlook as it now is, to claim that the new expedient is destined to become accepted as a settled standard in the terms of awards in displacement of the anti-bans clause, for purposes of dealing with the elusive question of strikes and work stoppages in employment.

It may be surmised that any success achieved by the application of the new method will not be limited to the object for which it was primarily adopted—namely, the defeat of industrial conduct not consistent with the requirements of awards, and the suppression of wanton interference with production or other forms of industrial lawlessness. The operation of this procedure should be the means of administering a check of some consequence to the intrigues and machinations of irresponsible multiunion shop committees and area committees.[66] As has been indicated, it should also have effects of note on the standing of the shop steward in the trade union, and throughout industry generally.[67]

It looks as if, in the normal case, the form of the provision as it appears in clause 6 of the Aluminium Industry Award (which was made by Mr Senior Commissioner Taylor), will be taken as the model where it is decided to import a settlement of disputes provision into an award—for example, clause 42 of the Transport Workers (Oil Companies) Award, 1964, made by Mr Commissioner Gough, copies clause 6 of the Aluminium Industry Award very closely in material respects, albeit the proviso in relation to dangerous working conditions is omitted.[68] This would mean that, subject to certain reservations, a requirement that work shall continue in the normal way of the establishment, while the procedural steps delineated in the settlement of disputes clause are being followed, will usually be adopted where a decision is made to include the provision in an award. Such a development should help to win greater confidence in the provision on the part of employers, and serve to reconcile them to the dropping of the anti-bans clause as a constituent of awards in the case of a greater number of industries.

Legislative Prevention of Ill-considered Resort to Industrial Sanctions

Late in the year 1964 a notable concession was made to labour demands on the question of penalties, in their relation to industrial strikes, when legislation amending the Industrial Arbitration Act, 1940-1961 of New South Wales, came into force.

---

[66] See p. 79.   [67] See pp. 71-3.

[68] Clause 36 of the Storemen and Packers (Oil Companies) Award, 1964, too, also made by Mr Commissioner Gough, incorporates a settlement of disputes provision very similar to that of clause 42 of the Transport Workers (Oil Companies) Award, 1964. Specific mention is made in the prescribed procedural arrangements of the part to be played by the shop steward (clause 36), and that to be played by the 'union delegate' (clause 42). See also pp. 90-3.

The new measure provides, *inter alia*, that no proceedings for an order under section 100 of the Act (as amended under its terms) shall be commenced without leave of the Industrial Commission of New South Wales. This section stipulates that, where in an industry a strike occurs that is illegal within the meaning of section 99 or section 99A of the Act, the Commission may order any trade union registered as an industrial union of employees whose executive or members are taking part in, or aiding or abetting, or have taken part in, or aided or abetted, the strike to pay a fine not exceeding the sum of £500.

The leave will not be granted unless the Commission is satisfied that the employer concerned in the illegal strike has (a) not himself taken part in any lock-out which has either wholly, or in part, given rise to the strike; (b) in a case where a lock-out or strike has taken place, notified the Registrar (appointed under the Act) in accordance with section 25A of the Act of the commencement of the lock-out or strike, or upon becoming aware of any question, dispute or difficulty of the nature referred to in paragraph (a), (b) or (c) of section 25(1) of the Act which gave rise to the strike, notified the Registrar in accordance with section 25A of the question, dispute or difficulty; and (c) to the extent to which the circumstances permitted, made a bona fide attempt to negotiate a settlement of the question, dispute or difficulty which gave rise to the strike before the strike took place, or of the strike after it had taken place. Furthermore, the leave will be refused unless the causes of and the circumstances that gave rise to the question, dispute or difficulty have been investigated or adjudicated upon by some industrial tribunal other than the Commission, or where the causes and circumstances have not been so investigated or adjudicated upon, the Commission itself has investigated the causes and circumstances.

The amending Act further provides that it is a defence to any proceedings under section 100 that (a) an employer in the industry in which the illegal strike occurred, or his servant or agent, has by any unjust or unreasonable action provoked or incited the strike; or (b) the executive of the union, after becoming aware of the circumstances concerning the illegal strike, has not aided, abetted or supported or did not aid, abet or support members of the union who are or were engaged in the strike, and has endeavoured or did endeavour by means reasonable in the circumstances to prevent members of the union from taking part in, or aiding or abetting, or continuing to take part in, aid or abet, the strike.

Costs, moreover, are not to be awarded in these illegal strike proceedings, or in applications for leave to proceed under section 100, and so cannot be sued for and recovered even though the prosecuted trade union has been found guilty and convicted on a summons for an illegal strike.

It will thus be seen that, as a prerequisite to the invocation of section 100, specified conditions must have been fulfilled by the employer involved, and an inquiry conducted to ascertain relevant facts, or an adjudication made upon them, by an industrial tribunal; the defence pleas, too, to proceedings under the section are added to and strengthened, with orders for costs disallowed. These changes lend increased emphasis to conciliation as a method for the prevention and settlement of labour disputes, and are calculated to encourage a fuller use of the available conciliation machinery before it is decided to seek the imposition of penalties. In other words they can be said to offer a degree of protection against hasty or ill-considered resort to a penal procedure where it is alleged that the continuity of production in an employment has been broken, or interfered with, as the result of trade union activity. Satisfaction from the application and working of the provisions may influence developments in the controversy surrounding the presence, or insertion, of the anti-bans clause in awards made under the Conciliation and Arbitration Act 1904-1964, and lead to the taking of steps that could serve to mitigate the bitterness associated with the conjoint operation of sections 109 and 111 of the statute.

Australian Industrial Tribunals' Interest in the Appointment of Shop Stewards

Australian industrial tribunals have shown a desire that shop stewards should be allocated to the workshops and job sites, where their function is deemed applicable. Accordingly, in such circumstances they have encouraged the appointment of suitable persons to these assignments, and sometimes have stipulated by award that, where an appointment of a shop steward made by the appropriate union is not acceptable to the employer concerned, employees themselves are to have the opportunity to bring complaints in relation to their work to the notice of management through a fellow worker nominated by themselves. Thus in the Furnishing Trades Award, 1964 (clause 37), there is included a provision to the effect that, where the appointment of a shop steward by the interested union—the Federated Furnishing Trade Society of Australasia—is not approved or recognized by an employer or his representative, a delegate chosen by and from the employees in the shop or factory in question is to have the necessary time during working hours to interview the employer or his representative at the shop or factory for the purpose of submitting grievances arising out of the employment.

The industrial tribunals are conscious of the desirability of maintaining facilities for quick and easy communication at every possible level and at every possible stage between workers and management. They see in such circumstances a stimulus to higher levels of industrial productivity, and to the establishment and preservation of good relations between workers and management that should render unnecessary any resort to direct action in the enforcement of industrial claims. But where, by their awards, they have provided for the recognition of accredited shop stewards by the employer and for the right of these shop stewards to interview the employer or his representative on employment matters, as specified, the tribunals have been at pains to see that the legitimate interests of the employer are not unduly prejudiced by the exercise of the right to interview. For instance, in terms of awards governing the textile industry it is stipulated that, while shop stewards 'to the number of one in each department' are to be recognized by the employer, not more than three of such shop stewards are to be allowed time off during working hours for the purpose of interviewing the employer where there is any legitimate complaint to discuss.[69] The provision can be said

[69] See clause 31 of the Textile Industry (Knitting Section) Award, of the Textile Industry (Woollen and Worsted Section) Award, of the Textile Industry (Cotton, Etc., Section) Award, of the Textile Industry (Man-Made Fibres Section) Award, and of the Textile Industry (Miscellaneous Sections) Award. All these awards, although sectional, are independent of each other, and were made in 1963. See also O. de R. Foenander, *Industrial Regulation in Australia*, p. 18.

to exemplify the acknowledgment by those responsible for the administration of the industrial law that the national well-being can be adequately served only when protection is forthcoming for employers, as well as for those whom they employ.

Further Usefulness of the Shop Steward to Trade Unionism

Not the least of the services that the shop steward can be expected to contribute to the progress of the trade union movement, and its endeavours to secure a better working life for employees, is informing union executives of what the ordinary members are thinking in reference to topics related to these matters—on the various policies of the union and methods of achieving the objectives of those policies, and conditions and problems in the particular industry in which they are employed. There seems to be a disposition—not altogether uncommon, it would appear—to ascribe practically the entire fund of industrial intelligence located in a trade union to its leaders, without serious consideration having been devoted to the question of capability and industrial experience of the generality of the members. In their association with their superiors in the union the shop stewards, who have their hands unceasingly on the pulse of events in the shop, are in a position to do much to dispel such a notion—baseless, it may be asserted, certainly for many years past. The ideas that generate in the minds of the rank and file members of the union should derive added validity with the growing strength of the new educational movement (in both its popular and technical aspects). Furthermore it can be said that, in the measure in which increasing notice is taken of the views of the many in the administration of union affairs, greater effect will have been given to one of the principal aims and purposes underlying the Australian industrial regulative systems—that trade unions registered under the provisions of the arbitration legislation will act in conformity with democratic practices, and so ensure a full recognition of the wishes of the majority of their members.[70]

The training of the shop steward in the art of unobtrusive

---

[70] Cf. the policy statement of the A.C.T.U. Congress that it 'affirms the right of a Trade Union to conduct its own affairs in its own democratic manner'—*Decisions of the Australian Congress of Trade Unions, 4-8 September 1961*, p. 14.

noting of happenings in the workshop, and recording what has been ascertained in this way in carefully arranged reports for submission to the appropriate branch or other executive of the union, should be of considerable assistance in the facilitation of trade union administration, as well as a factor of significance in its effectiveness. It might help further if the reports were to be compiled in accordance with a predetermined plan and lodged at regular or stated intervals, except on occasions when information on some matter of consequence is required without delay. Along with immediate notification to union officials of any sign of unaccountable undercurrents of restiveness among operatives, especially where it is suspected that they have their origins in some outside source, such activity on the part of the shop steward could be of importance in thwarting schemes, hatched by bodies not recognized by official trade unionism, for a sudden 'walk-off' from the job. It should, of course, have an added value where the organized 'lightning strike', as it is sometimes called, involves workers who are engaged in a key production unit of the factory or establishment.

NOTES TO THE CHAPTER

(1) *Australian Congress of Trade Unions and Trade Union Education, 1961*

The decision was expressed as follows:

The present age is one of rapid progress and this, together with the high rate of technological development demands that all sections of Commerce and Industry must be adequately equipped to meet the requirements of this modern age.

Congress is mindful that benefits can be conferred by Trade Union education and workers can be moulded into a united force capable of furthering the interests and improving the standard of living of workers generally.

The employing section of the community is training its representatives to combat the work of the Trade Union Movement in achieving its objectives. Congress declares that education in Trade Union objectives and Trade Union practices is essential. The complexities of industrial legislation and the extension of automotive processes in industry cannot be effectively understood by day to day practical experience only. Therefore, it becomes a vital necessity for present and future Trade Union officials to further their knowledge of these activities. Further, having in mind that it is essential to train as well as learn by experience, Congress decides:

(1) That a knowledge of the history of the Australian Labour Movement is essential in order that the rising generation of unionists may be able to understand and appreciate the struggles, trials and tribulations of the pioneers who, by their efforts laid a foundation for the conditions that obtain in industry today.

(2) That education in Trade Union practices and training in Trade Union activity is essential in order that from within our own ranks future leaders may be chosen who will be adequately equipped to efficiently perform the necessary functions on behalf of the Trade Union Movement.

(3) The wages and conditions of workers are largely governed by the economic condition of our country and it is necessary that the Trade unionists should have the knowledge to examine and understand economic trends and social change.

We therefore recommend to Congress that the Executive be authorized to set up a Committee to devise ways and means of furthering working class education in accordance with these principles.[71]

(2) *The Graphic Arts Case*

In the most recent case of its kind, it was asserted by the union involved that the dismissal of an employee from his job was an act of victimization, at the expense of one who was the union shop steward at the time in the establishment concerned. Mr Portus, a member of the Commission, held that the reason why the employee had been singled out for retrenchment was his activities as a shop steward, and, in consequence, was of the opinion that it was 'fair' that the steward should be reinstated in his previous employment. He accordingly requested the employer to do so. There was no claim, in argument in the case, for preferential treatment of any nature for a shop steward, as such, in any scheme for labour retrenchment in the establishment. The decision of the Commissioner rested solely on the ground that, in the choice of a person for a planned lay-off which, as the Commissioner agreed, was justified in the financial circumstances of the establishment, discrimination had been practised against the shop steward because of his activities as a delegate of a registered organization directed to the betterment of industrial

71 See *Decisions of the Australian Congress of Trade Unions, 4-8 September 1961*, p. 14.

conditions in the establishment. Section 5(1) of the Act provides a protection for officers, delegates and rank and file members of a registered organization against dismissal or injury at the hands of their employers in their employment, on account of industrial actions as specified in the terms of the sub-section.[72]

In a previous case—*Cairns Meat Export Co. Pty Ltd* v. *Australasian Meat Industry Employees' Union*—it was claimed that a man employed as a trimmer at the works, and who was also a union representative, had been selected for discharge when under economic exigencies it was found necessary to cut down staff in the establishment; the principal ground for the dismissal, it was alleged, was his continued representations to management on behalf of his workmates for improved conditions of employment. It was submitted, in defence, that the standard of efficiency shown by the complainant in the performance of his duties, and his attendance record on the job, did not warrant his retention in employment in preference to others who had not received notice and that his union activities were not a consideration when it was decided to put him off. Mr Findlay, of the Commission, took his stand on the principle, invariably observed by the industrial tribunals, that the furtherance of trade union business in a factory must not be allowed to interfere unduly with the effective conduct of its operations. He agreed that the demands made by the union on the complainant's working time exceeded the limits that an employer can fairly be expected to permit in according recognition of the rights of an accredited union representative, and that the complainant's output was below that of others retained in employment in the same section of the establishment. The question of any priority or privilege for an employee, *qua* union representative, was not raised at the hearing, and the Commissioner was careful to make clear his views on this matter, by remarking that a union representative 'is like any other employee on the payroll so far as his contract of employment is concerned'.[73] He decided to direct the company to re-employ the dismissed man in another section of the works, with the understanding that he should restrict himself within

[72] *In the matter of the Graphic Arts (Interim) Award, 1957 and In the matter of a Dispute between the Printing Industry Employees' Union and John Haigh Engravers Pty Ltd* (1963), not reported. See also p. 65.
[73] (1962) 100 C.A.R., at 549.

reasonable and legitimate limits when carrying out union business with respect to the establishment.

In another case—*Federated Liquor and Allied Industries Employees' Union of Australia* v. *Tooth & Co. Ltd*—where the ground for dismissal of a motor-lorry driver, who was a delegate of the union as well, was given by the company as his frequent late arrivals at delivery points and returns to the depot after the deliveries, the union suggested that the real reason for the dismissal was that the man was the holder of a position in the union. The submission was rejected by Mr Austin, of the Commission, who took the occasion to remind the parties that a delegate of a union is enabled to act in such a capacity only when he has entered into a contract of employment, and that he is an employee 'whose justification for employment is in the performance of duties, for which he is engaged, to the satisfaction of the employer'.[74] He found that the company was entitled to consider, on the facts, that the man had proved to be unsatisfactory in relation to its requirements as to the performance of his job, and accordingly upheld its action in terminating his employment.

(3) *Settlement of Disputes in Goodyear Tyre and Rubber Co. (Australia) Ltd, Shell Refining (Australia) Pty Ltd, and the Pulp and Paper Industry*

In *Goodyear Tyre and Rubber Co. (Australia) Ltd* v. *Federated Rubber and Allied Workers' Union of Australia*, Mr Austin, of the Commission, adverted to the problem of avoiding a stoppage of work, in circumstances where a dispute has arisen between management and employees, pending a settlement of the matter or matters in issue. In an order made in this case he laid down a formula of ways and means as a method for dealing with the problem. The provision is binding on one employer only, namely, the Goodyear Tyre and Rubber Co. (Australia) Ltd, and only in respect of working conditions and/or rates of pay in the company's works. It is expected, however, that it will be embodied in the next general award to be made in regulation of the rubber, plastic and cable-making industry, and will thus become binding on all employers who are parties to the award.[75]

74 (1963), not reported.
75 The current award in this industry was made in 1957, and is officially

The formula takes the shape of a succession of steps as follows:

(1) The dispute is to be submitted in writing to the appropriate executive—i.e. the foreman or supervisor—who must then give the employee concerned an official notification that he has received the complaint.

(2) The management is bound to arrange for the holding of a conference within two working days, after the receipt of the complaint, the parties to be represented by equal numbers from the union and the company. The number of representatives from each side is not to exceed six, and it is incumbent on the union to advise the company, prior to the commencement of the conference, of the size of its representation.

(3) If the conference proves fruitless, the matter in dispute is to be formally submitted by the appropriate State secretary of the union to the employer, to be dealt with at a future conference which must be arranged within one week of the receipt of the notification.

(4) In the event of the matter being still not settled at the close of the second conference, the issue is to be submitted by the federal secretary of the union to the Commission, whose decision is final and binding on the parties.

The order further provides that while the procedure as prescribed is being observed, work is to continue as required by the employee in accordance with the relevant award, without prejudice to the final settlement of the dispute.[76]

It will be observed that the formula makes no specific mention of the shop steward, and defines or assigns no part for him, as such, in the scheme that it outlines. But it will be realized that there are opportunities for this person to figure significantly in the first step of the arrangement described, and possibly later as one of those nominated to represent the union at a conference with the company where it is necessary that a meeting be held. Fellow-workers in the shop would be expected, as a matter of course, to turn to him for advice or assistance—for example, in the preparation of the statement of their grievances required for presentation to the foreman, or other appropriate representa-

---

known and referred to as the Rubber, Plastic and Cable Making Industry Award, 1957.

[76] (1963), not reported.

tive of management, in accordance with the procedure ordered to be observed. It may be remarked that a complaint by a shop steward employed by the company, arising out of an interview between himself and a division foreman in connection with his (the shop steward's) time-sheet for the previous day, was the occasion of the dispute in the determination of which the Commissioner prescribed his formula in relation to future disputes in the works; when satisfaction of the claim was refused, the men, under pressure from and at the instigation of the shop steward, ceased work. Their action evidences the probability that the shop steward would be called upon to share in any approaches made in the initial stage of the procedure, directed to be followed in terms of the order of the Commissioner.

Of interest, too, is the provision in an *agreement,* in operation, between one of the oil-refining companies and its employees for the settlement of disputes and claims at the company's works with regard to wages and conditions of employment. Known as the Oil Refinery Employees (Shell Refining (Australia) Pty Ltd) Agreement, it has been certified under the provisions of section 31(2) of the Act and therefore by virtue of that subsection has, as between the parties to the agreement, the same effect as, and is deemed to be, an award for all the purposes of the Act. Clause 21 of the agreement provides that, subject to the Act, any dispute or claim shall be dealt with in the following manner:

(1) The matter in dispute, or which forms the subject of the claim, is to be submitted by the shop steward to the Industrial Relations Officer or other appropriate officer of the employer.

(2) If not settled it is to be formally submitted by the State secretary, or other appropriate official of the union, to the employer.

(3) If still not settled it is to be submitted to a member of the Commission, whose decision is final and is to be accepted by the parties.

It is further provided that, while this procedure is being observed, work is to continue normally where it is agreed that there is a relative existing custom, while in other cases the work is to go on at the direction of the employer; no party, however, is to be prejudiced with respect to a final settlement of the dis-

pute, or claim, by the continuance of operations in the works
in terms of this provision.

The formula for the settlement of disputes or claims prescribed
in clause 36 of the Pulp and Paper Industry Agreement, 1961,
except in one noteworthy particular, is closely similar in substance to that contained in the corresponding clause in the agreement in relation to the Shell Refining (Australia) Pty Ltd (clause
21). As in the case of clause 21, the responsibility for making
the initial move towards a settlement in pursuance of clause 36
rests with the shop steward (albeit, in clause 36, an alternative
to action by the shop steward—namely, by 'other appropriate
officer of the union'—is specified), and, as in the case of the latter
agreement, the provisions in the relative clause for the settlement
of disputes or claims are declared to be subject to the Act, and
the agreement has been certified in accordance with the terms
of section 31(2) of the Act. The parties to the Pulp and Paper
Industry Agreement are the Amalgamated Engineering Union
(Australian Section) and other unions on the one part, and the
Australian Paper Manufacturers Ltd and other employers on the
other part. The variation or divergence from the other agreement
alluded to lies in the introduction of a further step in the procedure laid down; where the dispute or claim has not been settled
at the stage where it has been dealt with by the State secretary
of the union and the employer, the matter is to be discussed
between representatives appointed by the employer and the
federal committee of management of the union or unions concerned. It is not until there is a failure at this point that the
matter is to be referred to a member of the Commission for a
decision. There is, as will have been seen, an omission of any
such provision in the agreement governing the settlement of
disputes or claims arising out of employment at the works of the
Shell Refining (Australia) Pty Ltd—no requirement of a meeting
between employer representatives and the federal committee of
management of the union or unions concerned.

(4) *The Right of an Employer under Section 119*
for Alleged Breach of an Award

There is nothing to prevent an employer who is party to an
award from suing for, and recovering, a penalty under section

119 of the Act from an employee organization that is also bound by the award, on a claim that the organization is guilty of a breach or non-observance of a term of the award. The penalty that may be imposed, under the section, cannot exceed the maximum penalty provided by the award for a breach or non-observance of one or more of its terms or, in the absence of such a provision, the maximum penalty that the Commission is empowered to fix for a breach or non-observance of a term of an award. This maximum is specified under section 41 of the Act as £100 in the case of an organization. Under section 120 the Court —or any other court with authority to impose a penalty for breach or non-observance—may order that the penalty, or part of it, be paid into the Consolidated Revenue Fund, or to such organization or person as is specified in the order. The courts invested with jurisdiction to impose the penalty are named in section 119. Incidentally, the intendment of section 119 is, in the opinion of Spicer C.J., not to create an offence, or to empower the making of a conviction for an offence; where it is found that an award has been broken or not observed, the authority granted under the section in this connection is limited to the imposition of a penalty.[77] It can be said to be settled law that a proceeding under the section for breach or non-observance of an award is not a prosecution for an offence in relation to which a conviction may be entered and recorded—it is civil in nature and, in fact, an action for penalties.[78] There is, as the Full Industrial Court said in *Telegraph Newspaper Company Pty Ltd* v. *Australian Journalists' Association,* 'a clear distinction in law between a penal statute which imposes a penalty and a criminal enactment which creates a fine'.[79]

In all probability, the principal reason why employers usually favour the procedure under section 109 in preference to that under section 119 in cases of alleged breach of award or non-observance, is that a more severe penalty is available for imposition by the Court under section 111 for contempt of its authority in disregarding any order that it may make under section 109,

[77] See *Parkinson* v. *Grazcos Co-operative Ltd* (1958) 1 F.L.R., at 96.
[78] See *The King* v. *Associated Northern Collieries* (1910) 11 C.L.R., at 742.
[79] (1962) 3 F.L.R., at 43-4. See also *Australasian Meat Industry Employees' Union* v. *Thomas Playfair Pty Ltd* (1962) 3 F.L.R. 234.

than under section 119 for a proved infringement or non-observance of an award. The Court is enabled to impose a penalty of up to £500 in the case of an employee organization, in respect of a contempt consisting of a failure to comply with this order. Another reason for the preference that carries weight with employers is the hope that an order made under section 109 will be obeyed, making any step in pursuance of section 111 unnecessary, and opening up the way for the restoration of good labour relations forthwith. The order itself, it will be observed, is not in the nature of a penalty, and does not necessarily operate as such. In *Commonwealth Steamship Owners' Association* v. *Waterside Workers' Federation of Australia,* Dunphy J. said: 'It should be emphasized that orders under this section have no immediate punitive sanction. If the party enjoined obeys the order that is the end of the matter and no penal consequences follow as long as the directions of the Court are obeyed.'[80] It may be pointed out that, if it is sought to obtain an order under section 109 restraining a breach of an award by an organization, it is not necessary to prove that breaches have, in fact, occurred; it is sufficient to show to the satisfaction of the Court that, by reason of threats made, or other conduct, there is a reasonable apprehension that breaches by the organization will be committed if an order is not made.[81]

[80] (1960), not reported.
[81] See *Broken Hill Proprietary Co. Ltd* v. *Seamen's Union of Australia* (1960) 1 F.L.R. 324.

Part II

4

SHOP COMMITTEES

Constitution

As in Great Britain workers shop committees in Australia came
into prominence for the first time in the days of World War I,
declining somewhat in importance in the years that followed but
reviving in strength during the period of World War II. As in
other countries, in accordance with what is to be expected, these
committees in their Australian environment are found for the
most part only in the larger industrial establishments. This is
true whether representation on these bodies is limited to a single
union, or extends to two or more unions whose members are
employed in the same establishment. The presence in some
establishments of workers who are members of unions, other
than the central union interested in the industry, is due primarily
to the need for craftsmen or other classifications of craftsmen,
and others, as employees in the industry. Although in principle
ancillary or auxiliary in the part that they play in output, they
are often in considerable numbers, maintaining a collective and
independent identification in separate unions—for example,
blacksmiths, engineers, boilermakers, moulders (metals), elec-
trical and sheet-metal workers, and clerks.[1] The shop committees
that attract the greatest public attention and generate the most

---

[1] 'The term "industry" is not a precise technical term. One industry sometimes overlaps into another industry. In my opinion, no absolute rule can
be laid down for determining the limits of a particular industry. The question
whether a principal industrial occupation belongs to one industry rather than
another cannot be decided merely by considering the nature of that operation
itself. For example, a clerk may be employed in the boot-making industry,
the coal industry, the transport industry, or almost any industry. The problems associated with the overlapping of craft and industrial unions are well
known, and have to be carefully considered by industrial authorities when
they are determining the terms of their awards. In my opinion, all the circumstances in each case must be taken into account.'—per Latham C.J. in
The King v. *Hickman and Others; Ex parte Fox and Another* (1945) 70
C.L.R., at 608.

anxiety in officials in the general body of Australian unions are those constituted of persons not drawn solely from one union, particularly where they are located in the heavy industries or governmental instrumentalities or projects—for example, steel plants, engineering works, ship building and dock yards, zinc and chemical works, oil refineries, electric lighting and power stations, abattoirs, bridge construction and maintenance, and arms and munition establishments of various kinds in connection with the country's defence provision.

Although ordinarily a shop committee is comprised of shop stewards only, there are instances where, under the rules of a union, these committees are to be elected, whenever practicable, in all establishments where its members are employed, the electors being the members of the union employed in the establishment —for example, the Australasian Meat Industry Employees' Union, and the Federated Moulders' (Metals) Union of Australia. Usually an Australian shop committee is equipped with an executive, chosen by the members of the committee to hold office on a yearly tenure, and composed of a president, vice-president and secretary, and sometimes an organizer and committee of management as well.

Legal Justification for Appointment

Actually there are comparatively few unions in Australia the rules of which mention, or make express provision for, the appointment of shop committees constituted of their own members, or provide for representation on shop committees of stewards from a number of unions in the industry in which their special or primary interests lie. As a matter of fact, it is not always easy from a scrutiny of the rules of a union to defend on legalistic grounds the existence and operation of these bodies. A generous interpretation of the text (including, in particular, those clauses setting out the objects of the union as well as those directly dealing with the subjects of shop stewards and shop committees), with heavy reliance on the principle of implication, in the author's opinion would have to be applied in a number of instances to meet a challenge to the validity of action taken to form, or join, a shop committee.[2] Events in the history of the

2 Cf. p. 42.

Plumbers and Gasfitters Employees' Union of Australia furnish a case in point. Although not authorized in express terms by the rules, holders of high office in this union believe from their reading of the rules that they are empowered to direct and encourage shop stewards of the union to share in the activities of appropriate shop committees representing all unions that have members employed in the establishment, and, where such committees do not exist, to aid in steps taken to form them where deemed desirable. Directions and encouragement to this effect have, in fact, been given by this union. Much the same can be said in relation to the Australian Builders' Labourers' Federation. It may, indeed, be supposed, in the case of more than one of the unions whose rules are silent on the question, that the attitude of the supreme authority of the union towards shop stewards who join shop committees of this type, or take the initiative in their formation, is tantamount to a condonation of a breach of the rules.

Value

Provided they proceed within the scope of their authority and the ambit of the objects of the labour movement in the country, there is little doubt that shop committees, like shop stewards acting in their individual capacity and observing the same precepts, are capable of much in furtherance of the welfare of the unions and their members, and of management. Shop stewards and shop committees are, in themselves, a natural development in the structure of the trade union, and the evolution of its function. Where redress from management for a grievance arising out of his employment is sought by a worker, a shop committee is often in a position to deal with the matter more effectively than if the worker were left to his own devices, or even than if the appropriate shop steward were to take action on the complaint, and being 'on the spot' to do so more expeditiously than if resort were had to machinery more central to the union.

Nevertheless, even when restricted in membership to a single union these bodies have not proved, by their conduct, to be altogether an unqualified success, as is seen in the experience of unions such as the Australian Boot Trade Employees' Federation. For although certain of the shop committees instituted by this union gave a measure of satisfaction in realization of its purposes, others afforded ample ground for disappointment and annoyance. Those responsible for the general administration of the union's affairs adjudged that some of the committees were attempting to encroach upon functions rightfully belonging to the branch secretary, provoking strife, *inter alia,* and causing difficulties in the course of relations between management and the branch.[3] As a result the union considered it advisable to disband the offending bodies, and acted accordingly; indeed, after a while, the life of the remainder of the bodies came to an end. At the present time the union shows little disposition to look with favour on suggestions for the re-introduction of the committees. It has fallen back on methods in accordance with which a 'shop president' (as he is called under the rules of the union)[4] negotiates with an employer's agent or delegate on matters in issue in the factory, and duly reports the results of the discussions to the branch secretary as information to be brought before a meeting of the branch.[5]

Fears with regard to Multi-union Shop Committees

As indicated, it is in regard to the activities of multi-union shop committees—the form of job organization not in the nature of a gathering limited to representatives of one only of the unions with members who are employed in the establishment —that real apprehension is felt. These bodies as units are not within the jurisdiction or subject to the control of any individual union, because the powers of a union have no full appurtenance to shop committees not constituted solely of its own members. The *Report of Proceedings at the 92nd Annual Trades Union Congress, 1960,* stated: 'Each union can allocate a sphere of responsibility for its own stewards for no union individually is in a position to bring within its rules the joint committee of stewards from several unions or the officers of such joint

---

[3] The duties of shop committees, in the terms of the resolution adopted by the Federation authorizing their formation, were 'to look after the general welfare of members, and to negotiate through the Secretary, with approval of a Branch Meeting for improvements in amenities'.
[4] See p. 41.
[5] For the shop committee as a centre for the expression of discontent and ill-feeling against officials of the union, see O. de R. Foenander, *Trade Unionism in Australia* (Sydney, 1962), pp. 24-5.

bodies'.[6] The President of the Court of Arbitration of Western Australia, Mr Justice Nevile, in *Coastal District Committee, Amalgamated Engineering Union Association of Workers and Others* v. *Constructors John Brown and Others,* observed that these committees have

obviously no authority from the unions, as obviously no one of the unions having members working on the job can allow action to be decided by some committee composed largely of members of other unions to involve its members in action which may lead quite probably to the deregistration of the union.[7]

In the case of some of them, in fact, little is known of the actual method and circumstances of their appointment or election. It is not surprising, therefore, that fears are entertained —and industrial events in both Australia and beyond her shores have justified the reasonableness of such apprehensions—that these bodies will overstep the bounds of their authority and act in a manner displeasing to a union or unions represented on them, or in pursuit of objectives opposed to the principles for which the union or unions stand. Not infrequently, indeed, they have taken up an industrial issue with management in a militant way, without the knowledge or consent of the union most directly concerned or whose affair it primarily is, and industrial trouble has ensued. There is always the danger that, by their pronouncements and actions, they will implant untrue impressions of labour's intentions in the public mind, and discredit the good name of the trade union movement in the eyes of the community.

These committees in many instances betray an inclination to magnify petty grievances and minor differences in the establishment into wrongs and disputes of a major stature, and to arrogate to themselves the right to speak for organized labour in dealings with the employer. Developments of this nature can end in one way only—the undermining of the authority of responsible union and labour leaders and the infliction of irreparable damage upon the Australian industrial regulative system to which the continued existence of a strong and healthy trade unionism is fundamental.[8]

6 Op. cit., p. 128.
7 *Western Australian Industrial Gazette,* vol. 43, no. 3 (1963), p. 701.
8 O. de R. Foenander, *Wartime Labour Developments in Australia* (Melbourne, 1943), p. 105.

Entities such as these, in comporting themselves in this manner
and abusing the purpose for which avowedly they were created,
cannot expect to escape general condemnation as excrescences
menacing a healthy growth in the trade union movement.[9]

In Australia some unions realize the potentialities resident in
shop committees for co-ordinating the efforts of all shop stewards
in the establishment, irrespective of the union to which they
belong, thereby enhancing the prospect of obtaining better working conditions throughout the establishment for their own members as well as for the members of other unions employed in the
establishment, and they have adopted a policy of selectivity towards these committees based on the criterion of behaviour.
They would allow, and even encourage, their stewards to join
these committees in establishments where the conduct of the
committee meets with their approval, and refuse the permission
where it is not to their liking. Generally speaking, unions that
discriminate in this way do not hesitate to withdraw their representatives where the attitude of a shop committee changes in
favour of Communism, although there are cases where the association has been tolerated, and continued, as long as the Communism remains in the incipient or doctrinaire stage, and the
committee refrains from initiating or embarking upon a course
of action in contravention of the official aims of the union. It
should be understood, however, that by no means are all of
these shop committees in Australia given to Communist inclin-
ations or tendencies, and that even those that are Communist-
dominated are sometimes at pains not to follow plans or take
decisions calculated to antagonize unions whose stewards participate in their membership. Other unions, more conservative
in their outlook or less prepared to take risks, avoid the need
for, or pressure upon, their representatives to share in the activities of the committees by relying upon paid organizers attached
to the industry, or on a sub-branch specially assigned to the
industry. They would seem to be unattracted by the proposition
that close association, with joint discussion of shop stewards belonging to the various unions which have members employed in

9 'Shop stewards committees which become in effect unofficial bodies super-
imposed on the trade unions serve no useful purpose', says Harry Welton,
The Trade Unions, the Employers and the State (London, 1960), p. 117.

an establishment is likely to reduce inter-union misunderstanding and conflict in that establishment to a minimum.

Charter for Shop Committees, Constitution and Rules

In latter years the Australian Council of Trade Unions, which as the collective spokesman for the generality of Australian trade unions can be regarded as a counterpart of the American Federation of Labor-Congress of Industrial Organizations in the United States and the Trades Union Congress in Great Britain, has disclosed a sense of more than passive reservation in its consideration of the problem of the shop committees. From time to time it has, in fact, expressed strong dissent from decisions of shop committees of the multiple type, and on occasions has reprimanded them and denounced the trend of their industrial policy. As a means of containing the activities of these bodies within the limits of what it conceives to be sound union policy, the Australian Congress of Trade Unions in September 1961 adopted a number of articles together intituled 'Charter for Shop Committees, Constitution and Rules'. As the Congress is the governing body of the general trade union movement in Australia, the document can be said to embody a declared policy of Australian trade unionism.[10] The hope was entertained that this instrument would be accepted and observed as a blue-print or guide by those of its affiliated unions whose shop stewards join, or take a hand in the formation of, this class of committee. The Charter makes a series of recommendations in relation to these committees, and sets them out under seven heads, namely, constitution, representation, functions, officers, meetings, quorum, and control.

With regard to constitution, the Charter advises that a committee should consist of representatives of all unions that have members employed in an establishment. Each such union, it is urged, should elect its representatives from its own members in the establishment and, preferably, they should be shop stewards; the representatives should be elected at a meeting convened for the purpose of members of the union. Where,

[10] The Congress may be described as the legislature of the movement, and the A.C.T.U. as the executive. See O. de R. Foenander, *Trade Unionism in Australia*, pp. 12-14. The Charter is sometimes referred to as the A.C.T.U. Charter for Shop Committees, or simply as the A.C.T.U. Charter.

however, this course is deemed to be 'impracticable because of the disproportion of membership in the various departments', it is suggested that the matter should be referred by an appropriate union, or unions, to the branch of the A.C.T.U. in the State or district concerned for a variation to meet the particular needs of the establishment. The intention underlying this alternative, it may be presumed, is to enable representation on a shop committee—probably on a more or less proportional basis—to be afforded to relatively small groups of employees, such as maintenance workers, who are strongly outnumbered by production operatives in the establishment and by the application of their numerical strength alone, cannot hope to attain to any such representation.

In the view of the Congress, the functions of a committee should be the promotion of a sentiment of unity among the members of the various unions in the respective establishments for the purposes of (a) dealing with questions of improvements in shop conditions that affect more than one union; (b) assisting, when requested by the union concerned, to gain better shop conditions peculiar to the department in which members of this union are employed; and (c) collaborating with other shop committees to obtain improvements in general workshop conditions throughout the entire establishment. The Charter, however, reminds affiliates that anything affecting wage rates and conditions of employment covered by an industrial award or industrial agreement is—by constitutional necessity—a matter for decision by the union or unions concerned, and no affair of a shop committee.

It is advocated that the officers of a shop committee should be a president, a vice-president and a secretary, and that they be elected at a meeting summoned for the purpose of members of the respective unions in the establishments concerned, and thereafter at an annual meeting similarly called, with the same procedure observed with respect to the filling of vacancies as they arise. Meetings of these committees, the Charter adds, should be held at regular intervals, and at such meetings a quorum should be formed by a majority of the appointed union representatives.

Finally, under the plan embodied in this document all shop

committees should be subject, as to their decisions and actions, to the rules and conditions of the respective unions concerned; there would be no power vested in the shop committee to determine matters, or abrogate decisions, contrary to the rules and conditions of the respective interested unions, and the authority of a union over its shop stewards and other representatives would remain unimpaired and unaffected. These committees, moreover, would be under an obligation to comply with the procedures determined by the branch of the A.C.T.U. in the State in which the shop committee in question is located. 'Procedures', as used in this connection, means the industrial dispute practices and conduct generally that a trade union affiliated with the A.C.T.U. is bound to observe—more particularly, the requirement to notify the Disputes Committee of the appropriate State Trades and Labour Council of a threatened or impending industrial dispute, before proceeding to industrial action of any kind in relation to it.

Attention is drawn to the fact that there is nothing of a compulsive or mandatory character regarding the application of the Charter to any trade union, or shop committee (either existing or in the course of formation). Adoption or acceptance of its provisions is a purely voluntary step. No shop committee is forced to frame or amend its charter to make it agree with the substantive contents of the Charter, and no obligation is imposed on a trade union to direct its shop stewards, or delegates on a job site, to join an appropriate shop committee because the charter of that committee conforms with the recommendations of the Charter. It is a matter entirely within the discretion of the union itself to decide whether its representative in the workshop will become a member of any such committee, the extent to which he is to participate in the discussions and operations of a committee that he has been authorized to join, and whether and when any notice of discontinuance of membership of it shall be lodged and the adherence terminated.

Provisions of the A.C.T.U. Charter Copied

There is little in the nature of reliable information, known to the author, which indicates the number of shop committees whose charters conform with the recommendations of the

A.C.T.U. Charter for Shop Committees. But from all reports it can be said that relatively few shop committees have sought, successfully or otherwise, the formal endorsement of the appropriate State branch of the A.C.T.U. certifying that, in their case, the charter complies with the qualifying tests laid down in the A.C.T.U. Charter. Under its charter, however, a shop committee may well pursue policies that are, in fact, well within the coverage or objectives of the A.C.T.U. Charter, and still not seek recognition of any character from the A.C.T.U., or the respective A.C.T.U. State branch. Moreover there are shop committees, some of which had already been formed, that have deleted from their charters the reference to industrial matters. The amendments must have afforded considerable satisfaction to the A.C.T.U. and the generality of its affiliated trade unions, for where such steps have been taken the A.C.T.U. and these unions would have every reason to feel assured that the shop committees in question would follow a policy on industrial issues strictly in unison with that determined by the A.C.T.U. One of the principal reasons for the adoption of the Charter by the A.C.T.U. Congress was the prevention of unauthorized committees of any kind from being established, and proceeding to deal with industrial matters regarded as properly within the jurisdiction of the legitimate trade unions. Interestingly enough, it appears that for the most part shop committees, the provisions of whose charters are consistent with the criteria outlined in the A.C.T.U. Charter, are limited to federal government departments and instrumentalities. At the very least it cannot be denied that they are strongly represented in employments in these fields. But it would be wide of the truth to conclude, on that account, that there are not a number of industrial establishments of note in which there are to be found shop committees whose constitution and practice fully satisfy the essential demands and requirements of the Congress Charter.

Where, as would be expected, the charter of a shop committee has been endorsed by the apposite State branch of the A.C.T.U. as fulfilling the requirements of the A.C.T.U. Charter, it will be for the branch to sanction any alteration in the terms of the charter if the recognition of the A.C.T.U. is to continue. It is insufficient for the shop committee in question, or the interested trade unions, to effect any change without the approval of the branch, if it is desired that the recognition of the charter by the A.C.T.U. is to be maintained.

The Problem of the Area Committees

The Charter makes no attempt to deal with the vexed question of the shop area committees, but the opinion of the great majority of responsible union leaders is strongly adverse on the issue of association with them. These bodies have never had the endorsement or approval of the A.C.T.U. or its State branches, and are not recognized by them as a part or form of the official trade union organization; on the contrary, their activities are regarded by them as a threat to the integrity and solidarity of the labour movement. The A.C.T.U., on more than one occasion, has categorically warned its affiliated unions against the conduct of these committees and their like, and urged all members of the unions to observe the rules and procedures of their own unions and the State branches of the A.C.T.U. in the struggle for improvements in standards in employment, and to lose no opportunity of ensuring that the traditional rights and authority of the unions are not usurped or weakened in any way by the actions of these bodies.[11] No union in Australia, as far as the author is aware, has followed the example of the British Transport and General Workers' Union in making provision in its rules in relation to area committees.

Attitudes towards Multi-union Shop Committees and Area Committees

In previous years, particularly those of the earlier period of World War II, Australian employers were disposed to look with some favour on multi-union shop committees and shop area committees, and to recognize their existence and encourage their operation in their establishments. They indulged the hope that these bodies had a contribution to offer to the promotion and maintenance of industrial peace in the community. With the widespread disillusionment and disappointment in this respect that followed, however, employer organizations counselled their

[11] See pp. 122-5.

members to limit their negotiations on labour issues to the authorized representatives of the trade union or unions involved, or accredited delegates from organized trade unionism at a higher level, disregarding the approaches of shop and area committees except where made with the concurrence of trade union officialdom. Some of them, as a matter of fact, have repeatedly admonished their members, in unequivocal language, of the risks that they run in permitting the presence and activities of these bodies on their premises.

This attitude on the part of organized employers in latter days is shared by the community in general, which takes umbrage at the readiness of these bodies to precipitate worker groups into courses of militancy and direct action in support of industrial claims, and resents their attempts to prevail on operatives to ignore the instructions of their union executives in the prosecution of employment demands and the settlement of grievances in the shops and factories and on the job sites. This is not the outcome solely of a natural desire that industrial production shall continue, without dislocation or interruption, for the benefit of all; it is also in appreciation of the contributions that well-ordered trade unions have made to the national prosperity and well-being, and are expected to make in the years to come.

There appear, however, to have been a number of cases in recent days—greater, perhaps, than one has reason to expect—in which management has failed to exhibit more than a token resistance to the advances of multi-union shop committees and area committees, and has had dealings with these bodies without the knowledge, and almost certainly without the assent, of the union whose constitution associated it with the employment to which the matter in question was related. The promptings of a narrow self-interest would no doubt provide, in the last analysis, the actuating motive on most of these occasions—that is, a decision to take the easy way and avoid the loss or difficulties that a refusal to negotiate might seem to involve, or a calculation that, by the adoption of such a course, a competitive advantage of sorts over business or trade rivals might be gained. In other instances, the explanation may possibly lie in a dislike entertained towards the particular union or of its individual officers, or in some feeling of resentment engendered by the presence of unionism in industry, the standing that it enjoys under the industrial law, or the role that it occupies in the field of labour relations and other areas of communal affairs. Generally it is hard to avoid the conclusion that, except in the unusual case, the behaviour of employers who lend themselves to such practices is symptomatic of a poor social outlook on their part and of those who would be prepared to commend them in this attitude.

On occasions employers, by their hasty or ill-advised actions, have unwittingly played into the hands of these bodies and indirectly aided them in the furtherance of policies that indeed, if realized, could easily prove injurious to the best interests of the employers themselves. Such things may happen when a strike or stoppage of work having been called, or a restriction on the progress of operations declared, in the establishment they do not exercise the discretion or forbearance that could reasonably be expected of them before deciding to move for an order under section 109 of the Act; they fail to consider with care the particular facts, or special circumstances, of the individual case and to practise discrimination in dealing with situations of this kind. There have been too many instances in which the section has been invoked in relation to what, after all, are comparatively minor or inconsequential defaults, or where a reputable employee organization with a good record of industrial behaviour has been cited, under its provisions, to answer for the industrial misconduct of some of its members of which it wholly disapproves and in which it has had no hand.[12] Such cases stamp the employers concerned as deficient in the quality of distinguishing the essential from the non-essential, and lacking in the faculty of judiciously allowing matters of a lesser significance

12 A good example of an employer association that can be said, from the available evidence, to observe a policy of restraint in the matter of approaches to the Court under the section is the important and well-organized Metal Trades Employers' Association. This Association claims that it habitually explores every available opening for the practice of conciliation, as well as other methods, in the attempt to bring about an amicable settlement of an industrial dispute, making an application under the section for an injunction 'only as a last resort'. See the *Metal Trades Journal* (the official organ of this Association), vol. 30, no. 7 (15 April 1964), p. 187. The claim finds further expression in a later issue of the journal—vol. 30, no. 16 (1 September 1964), p. 472.

to pass without taking action—particularly where a recourse to the processes of the Court is involved.

A number of shop committees and area committees that are controlled by extremist opinion, it is believed, welcome applications under the section in the hope that they will be followed by the infliction of a penalty in pursuance of the provisions of section 111 of the Act.[13] It is suggested that, where possible, they bring pressure to bear on employee organizations that have become involved in these proceedings to refrain from any defence at the hearings under the sections, or, at the most, to submit arguments that are lacking in the elements of sincerity and soundness. The frequent imposition of fines by the Court and the granting of legal costs to accompany them could, of course, prove useful to these committees in their propaganda activity that endeavours to present a picture of the instrumentalities of labour regulation, in their operation in Australia, as machinery that drains away the financial resources of unions whose only sin is an enthusiastic devotion to the cause of the legitimate rights of their members. The committees that hold such views and apply such tactics are anxious to discredit this machinery, confident that the ultimate result will be its withdrawal or overthrow. Such a development would be favourable, no doubt, to the plans of those who are bent upon disruption in industry, and social subversion throughout the land.

There is reason to believe that the legal costs incurred by the unions in prosecutions under the 'penal provisions' of the Act, as they are often loosely styled—section 109 with its predecessor section 29, and section 111 with section 29A which it replaced under an amending enactment of 1956—are little less in amount, if at all, than the fines imposed on them in terms of orders made on summonses in pursuance of sections 29A and 111. The unions, in fact, declare that they are in excess. By the end of August 1964 the accumulated figure for the fines, as ascertained from official sources, had reached approximately £51,000. It is

13 See pp. 74-5 for some reference to the conjunctive operation of sections 109 and 111 of the Act—the seeking of an order, under section 109, enjoining an organization from continuing a breach or non-observance of an award, and, where made, the imposition under section 111 of a penalty on the organization, if found guilty by the Court of non-compliance with the order.

not governmental policy, or practice, to publish statistics show-
ing moneys received in settlement of these obligations, but it
can be said, generally speaking, that the unions are prompt in
the discharge of their penalty indebtedness, and that in no instance has it been found necessary to sue for the recovery of
these penalties. Reliable information is not easy to obtain with
regard to all of the amounts of costs where orders were made
under the provisions, or the extent to which these costs have
been satisfied to the present time, but in a statement made to the
Prime Minister, Sir Robert Menzies, and the Minister for
Labour and National Service, Mr William McMahon, in May
1964 by a representative delegation of the A.C.T.U., it was
revealed that, up to September 1963, sums totalling £33,000
had been paid out by the unions in the shape of costs owing by
them on account of orders made in accordance with the provisions.[14] The figure is much the same, in the author's conjec-
ture, as that for the fines as it stood on or about 30 June 1963.

The unions complain that only too often counsel is briefed
quite needlessly, to appear before the Court on behalf of employers—for example, in applications presenting no difficulties
of note, or in connection with matters of a purely formal character—and that there is little hesitation on other occasions about
engaging or retaining senior counsel when a junior could adequately undertake all that is required to be done. These practices, it is alleged, contribute substantially to the amounts that
the unions have had to find to cover the costs allowed against
them.

Officials of the unions have expressed anxiety at the impover-
ishing effects of the litigation and other legal expenses that their
organizations are forced to meet, and are particularly concerned
in this respect with the fines and costs arising out of proceedings in enforcement of the penal provisions. The A.C.T.U. has
had no compunction in charging employers with seeking to exploit the provisions for their own purposes—to the end of pro-
curing orders for the imposition of fines on the unions and
awards involving 'extortionate' costs against them. The accusa-
tion has been vigorously denied by employer representatives
who claim that, far from abusing the rights to which they are

14 See the *A.C.T.U. Bulletin* (Melbourne, June-July 1964), p. 2.

entitled under the Act and defeating the objects of this legislation, employers usually postpone the invocation of section 109
as long as there is a reasonable chance that the union at fault
will desist from its industrial wrongdoing, and that even when
an order is made under the section they refrain from further
action in prosecution until all hope that the union will see the
error of its ways has apparently completely disappeared. In de-
murring, they also aver that it is the aim of employers to lighten
the incidence of costs and other legal expenses resulting from
the proceedings for the payment of which the unions have become liable, to the greatest extent within their power.

It is pertinent to mention that the question of costs is one
within the discretion of the Court and that, in the exercise of
that discretion, the Court has at times made orders absolute or
imposed penalties, as the case may be, without any further
order for costs. There has also to be borne in mind the fact that
the grant of costs almost invariably provides for their taxation
by the appropriate Deputy Industrial Registrar appointed under
the Act who, when a bill for them is duly submitted for taxation, does not necessarily pass unamended what is marked on
counsel's brief, or otherwise sanction the full amount asked for.
This official may take the view that the engagement of 'expen-
sive' counsel was not justified in the circumstances and reduce
the amount of the bill accordingly, and he may refuse to authorize fees for more than one counsel, and disallow other items
as well. Often, as the result of an arrangement, the amount of
the costs is settled in conference by representatives of the parties
themselves, without any reference to the Deputy Industrial Registrar at all.

Resentment of the Trade Unions against
Area Committees

The warnings of the A.C.T.U. addressed to its affiliated
unions and their members against dealings with area committees
and bodies of that kind have, perhaps, a growing significance
in their application to shop stewards. Some of these persons, it
is asserted, have been subjected to considerable pressure at
times to be present at meetings of area committees, on the

agenda paper of which there are set down for discussion and decision matters that are claimed to be entirely the concern of the individual union. They suffer, too, according to reports, from a measure of embarrassment on occasions because of other forms of attention and importunity directed to them by the committees.

Trade union leaders are particularly incensed, understandably, when area committees are used, as they appear to have been not infrequently in recent days, as a means by which attacks can be levelled against their policies and activities and those of the A.C.T.U. and the various State Trades and Labour Councils. They take strong exception too, when, as is alleged, these committees strike levies on members of a union without its concurrence, for the pursuit of objects that it is argued are solely the affair of the union. But not the least of the annoyances of which they complain are those that arise from the invocations of these bodies to shop committees and workers to ignore resolutions and decisions of the union, and to disregard the provisions of industrial agreements between the union and employers, in some cases involving operatives in work stoppages that have not been authorized by the union. Of these stoppages the A.C.T.U. has, at times, made specific mention of those that have been brought about in the workshops through influences emanating from these outside sources. It is, indeed, difficult to escape the conclusion that, in more than a few instances, area committees have come to constitute a standing danger to peace in industry, making it impossible not to view them otherwise than in the light of an industrial nuisance.

Absence of Specific Provision Governing Shop and Area Committees in Industrial Awards

Members of shop committees and area committees in their individual capacities, like their fellow members in the trade union, are entitled to rights and subject to obligations under the terms of awards made in pursuance of the industrial arbitration law that are binding upon the organization to which they belong. Whereas, however, particular provision covering privileges and incidental reservations has been made in some awards with respect to shop stewards,[15] there is a total absence in the awards of any regulatory prescription in regard to these committees. The committees, as such, are unknown to the law and are without status under it, and they enjoy no recognition in the eyes of the industrial tribunals.

The Area Committee and the 'Alcoa Dispute'

Developments in connection with recent industrial differences in Western Australia, commonly referred to collectively as the 'Alcoa Dispute',[16] illustrate the embarrassment that area committees can cause to trade unions, employers and constituted authority, and the mischief that they can inflict on the interests of employees. Discontent had arisen among workers engaged in the construction of the alumina refinery in that State as regards terms and conditions of employment prescribed under the award by which they were governed—the Metal Trades Construction (Alumina Refinery) Award, 1962, made by the State Court of Arbitration. Demands in satisfaction of these grievances, either identical or substantially similar in effect, were made individually by job stewards representing the different classifications of men employed on the job on the various contractors and sub-contractors concerned, and when the employers refused to comply the job stewards formed themselves into what they called the 'Area Committee'. This body presented to the employers a list of demands much the same in character as those already made on them by the individual shop stewards, accompanied, it seems, by at least an implied threat that work on the site might be brought to a standstill if the requirements were refused. Apparently the employers either rejected the demands outright, or informed the men that the proper course would be for their unions to apply to the Employers' Federation, a body which was authorized to negotiate such matters on behalf of the employers involved. Negotiations between the unions and the Federation were, in fact, initiated, but their progress was interrupted by a stoppage of work on the job. An order was thereupon made by the Court of Arbitration directing a return

15 See pp. 67-8.
16 Alcoa is an abbreviation for Alcoa of Australia Proprietary Limited, an enterprise interested, in particular, in the mining, refining and smelting of aluminium.

to work under the provisions of the award, but although the order was obeyed and negotiations were resumed, workers resorted to 'go slow' tactics, working to safety regulations, and using other means of retarding industrial operations.

At length union officials were able to secure the support of a majority of the members of the Area Committee, and with their assistance managed to induce the men to abandon their dilatory and time-wasting methods and revert to recognized industrial practices, enabling an approach to be made for the application of the State industrial machinery in settlement of the issues in question. The President of the Court of Arbitration, Nevile J., nevertheless declined, in the circumstances, to convene a compulsory conference at the request of the unions, pending an adequate assurance that any settlement agreed upon at the proposed conference would be observed by all concerned. On the assurance being given and confirmed by a resolution passed at a mass meeting of the workers, the conference was summoned and duly held. The conference, however, was not successful, and when the failure was reported to the President, the matters in dispute were ordered to be referred into Court. The dispute was eventually determined by arbitration, the award being amended to provide for a rise in wage rates, an increase in site allowances and more favourable conditions of employment for employees on the job.[17]

The workers were loud in their complaints that there had been undue delay in the determination of the dispute, but the President did not hesitate to assert that for any delay that may have occurred the men had themselves 'largely to blame';[18] they had listened to the promptings of the Area Committee and disregarded the counsels of the unions. No culpability, the President believed, could attach to the union officials for the course that had been pursued by them. He said:

I am quite sure that neither the original stoppage nor the 'go slow' tactics were suggested or encouraged by the Union officials who, I am convinced, did everything they could to persuade the men to continue to work normally in accordance with the Award. But I

[17] *Coastal District Committee, Amalgamated Engineering Union Association of Workers and Others v. Forwood Johns Pty Ltd and Others* (1963), *Weste n Australian Industrial Gazette*, vol. 43, no. 2 (1963), p. 350.
[18] Ibid., p. 351.

am equally sure that these breaches of the Act and the Award would not have occurred without the encouragement and possibly the suggestion of the job stewards committee, although some individual job stewards may have done their best to assist their Union officials.[19]

In the opinion of the President the events of the dispute go to show 'quite clearly' that men who turn their backs on their union leaders and endeavour, without their aid, to force concessions from their employers, usually discover to their cost that, even though there may be substance in their claims, such 'misguided efforts' serve to postpone rather than hasten or facilitate the granting of these demands.[20] Negotiation in the real sense of the term, as he pointed out, is not practicable between a number of employers and a large body of job delegates; moreover, following the break-down of negotiations, an area committee is not in a position to request the calling of a compulsory conference under the Industrial Arbitration Act to discuss the dispute with a view to the reaching of an amicable agreement *inter partes,* because, unlike an industrial union registered under the terms of that Act, it has no standing before the Court. The result is that the attempt to apply direct pressure to employers

only prevents or delays the institution of proper negotiations between one or two representatives of the Unions and one or two representatives of the employers while if the matter has to be ultimately determined by this Court, no such determination can be requested until the Unions have full charge of the matter and can therefore speak with authority on behalf of the men concerned. Certainly this Court will not expedite the hearing of a dispute when it has reason to doubt whether one of the parties will accept its decision. Nor can it proceed to a hearing of any dispute while the party, claiming that the matter should come before the Court, is acting either in breach of the provisions of the Act under which the Court functions or in breach of an Award or Order made by the Court.[21]

In short, by observing the directions of an outside body in preference to the advice of their union leaders the men had deprived themselves, for a time, of the advantages of a proper bargaining technique, as well as the right to assistance from the constituted industrial authority in the realization of what they were seek-

19 Ibid., p. 350.   20 Ibid., p. 351.   21 Ibid.

ing. A measurable period had therefore to elapse before demands, shown to be legitimate in character, were granted.

It is noteworthy that the President was at considerable pains, in this case, to warn workers of the folly of passing over the leadership of the appropriate and properly constituted unions, and permitting the control of their affairs to fall into the hands of a body like an area committee, not qualified by its nature to handle such matters and not in a position to obtain for them the good offices of a tribunal in the just settlement of their claims.

Favourable Conditions for Multi-union Shop Committees and Area Committees

Past occurrences seem clearly to indicate that the formation of multi-union shop committees and area committees and the resurgence of activities by existing ones are more probable in an atmosphere in which workers have become restive, or grown discontented with what is being done on their behalf by union officials in furtherance of their industrial interests. Complaints against the union are frequently based on allegations of delay on the part of its officials in bringing key grievances, such as those in relation to wage rates and conditions of employment, to the notice of the industrial authorities or management, or failure to press these claims with vigour and enthusiasm at hearings before the industrial tribunals or in conferences with employers. Such circumstances are well suited to the prosecution of the aims and purposes of extremists and mischief-makers of all types, who see in the dissatisfaction of workers opportunities for stirring up feeling against union leaders and the resort to unorthodox courses of action to remedy neglects, imagined or otherwise.

With the strengthening of the influence of the A.C.T.U. throughout the generality of Australian trade unions and among the workers—enabling that body to approach, and deal with, its problems with greater confidence and increased determination— and a more widespread knowledge and appreciation in industry of the formulae contained in the Charter for Shop Committees, Constitution and Rules adopted by the A.C.T.U. Congress and recommended by it to the practice of affiliated unions, the multi-union class of shop committees should, however, be placed on sounder foundations and possibly severe limits imposed on the growth and activity of area committees. There would, of course, always remain a proportion of disgruntled workers ever prone to criticize, and complain, beyond all reason. A section of them seems to be given to obeying, almost without question at times, instructions from non-conforming multi-union committees and area committees, without affording serious thought to the views that the officers of their union may entertain on the matter under consideration. They apparently believe that the opinions of union leaders on labour issues between themselves and their employers are, in point of validity, quite secondary to those put forward by spokesmen for these committees. It is this class of persons who readily furnish, or form, the nucleus of a breeding ground for the reception and spread of misconceived industrial ideas, and the festering of illegitimate grievances with respect to employment activity.

Possibilities in a Linkage between Multi-union Shop Committees and the Trade Union Movement

There are distinct possibilities of advantage, to labour and enterprise alike, in a co-ordination of effort involving multi-union shop committees and general trade unionism. The difficulty, however, is how to establish the nexus, and furthermore how to maintain it in such a way as to exploit any benefits that such an arrangement may have to offer. Sir Walter Citrine was convinced of the prospect of beneficial results to follow the effecting of such a liaison. In a contribution to the *Sheffield Telegraph* a little over two decades ago he said:

Just as the shop stewards individually have proved of value to the separate trade unions, so the shop stewards committees rightly guided and linked up with the trade unions collectively can become not less serviceable to the trade union movement as a whole. There is no link between the shop stewards committee as such and individual trade unions. Nor is it easy to see how such a committee could have a direct connection with a particular union. Its members represent all the unions, and therefore if it is to function as a unit in discussions with the management it should have contact with somebody representing the interests of the unions as a whole. It is here that the difficulty arises. No such link has ever existed.[22]

In Australia little serious thought appears to have been devoted to the problem of harnessing the generality of multi-union shop committees to organized trade unionism, and certainly no step of a tangible nature has, as yet, been taken in this direction. Nor, seemingly, has there been any investigation of note into the advantages that could be expected to accrue from the institution of a working connection, or integration of some kind, involving the official trade union movement and these bodies.

Effective Internal Discipline in a Trade Union Movement

A high level of discipline within the trade union movement of a country, ensuring its orderly development, is generally regarded as essential if the maximum benefits that a movement of this kind is capable of affording are to be made available. To maintain the desired standards of discipline much depends on whether the movement is characterized by a close co-operation embracing and affecting the individual trade unions, and an effective control directed from the central authority. Another factor of significance is the measure in which the residence of powers, as they are distributed among the various trade union officers and position-holders, is readily ascertainable. It should, moreover, be an advantage if the constitutional structure or fabric of the different component unions were shaped as much as practicable according to a uniform pattern; this should render easier the detection of trespasses on the function of the supreme authority in the movement and on the domain of fellow-union affiliates, and facilitate the enforcement of decisions of a punitive nature that have been arrived at. Comprehensiveness, too, is important, and should include workers and their representatives, as well as other activists on their behalf, in the greatest degree possible.

As has been pointed out, there are bodies such as area committees exercising an influence on the course of relations between employers and employees in Australia which form no part

[22] See the issue of 26 November 1942. The passage is quoted in *British Trade Unionism—Six Studies* (Political and Economic Planning, London, July 1948), p. 131.

of the official labour organization in this country, and do not come within the scope of its authority.[23] To what extent, if at all, there is provision for internal discipline with respect to the conduct of the affairs of these bodies the author is unable to say. But ample evidence is forthcoming to show that, as long as they are not subject to the disciplinary jurisdiction of the A.C.T.U., limits are imposed to what can be achieved by organized labour in Australia to protect and further the interests of the working population, and those of the community as a whole.[24]

NOTE TO THE CHAPTER

Recent Resolutions of the A.C.T.U. Condemning Impingement Upon Trade Union Authority

Two recent resolutions of the Interstate Executive of the A.C.T.U., in condemnation of shop committees, area committees and other sections of workers that attempt to trespass upon the function of the legitimate trade union in the industrial movement, were carried in March 1962 and December 1963, respectively. As these decisions covered matters affecting the trade union movement as a whole, they were subject to the approval and endorsement of a majority of the State branches of the A.C.T.U.—that is, the State Trades and Labour Councils —as a condition precedent to their becoming operative. The necessary endorsements were secured, and they duly became an integral part of the official policy of the A.C.T.U. A third resolution on the question of shop committees, *inter alia*, was adopted by the Interstate Executive of the A.C.T.U. in September 1964. It has just received the formal acceptance and endorsement of a majority of the State Trades and Labour Councils, and its substance is now accordingly embodied in the official policy of the A.C.T.U.

The resolutions were expressed in the following terms:

(a) *The Resolution of March 1962*

This Executive views with concern reports from Victoria and N.S.W. indicating that Industrial Agreements recently agreed upon,

[23] See pp. 114-15.   [24] See pp. 116-19.

have been repeatedly broken by sections of workers without reference to the A.C.T.U., the Labour Councils or even individual Unions parties to the Agreement.

It is fundamental that where Unions enter into Agreements with Employers, these Agreements must be honoured by the parties. To the extent that Unions or their Branches or Membership whether incited by official or unofficial bodies or persons fail to so honour their undertakings, such failures are to be condemned.

Where Agreements are made under the auspices of the A.C.T.U. and there is a failure to abide by their terms, the A.C.T.U. will be compelled to consider whether it will continue to arrange Conferences between Employers and Unions for the purpose of arriving at Industry Agreements.

In some cases breaches of Agreements are arising from an excess of authority of Shop Committees and action by Area Committees and other forms of organisation not approved by the A.C.T.U. or Trades and Labour Councils.

The Executive, therefore, calls upon all Unionists to assist to preserve the integrity and solidarity of the Trade Union Movement by recognising only those forms of Trade Union organisation that have been approved by the A.C.T.U. or Trades and Labour Councils and to work for the improvement of the workers' standard only through the official Trade Union organisation.

To the extent that Shop Committees conform to the Charter that has been adopted by the 1961 A.C.T.U. Congress, they have an important function in the Trade Union Movement.

Recognising that there can be advantage to the Trade Union Movement by the co-ordinated effort of all Sections of Trade Unions, the Executive directs the Executive Sub-Committee to consider ways and means of achieving closer harmonious integration of Shop Committees with the official Trade Union Movement.

(b) *The Resolution of December 1963*

This Executive views with grave concern the actions of Area or Shop Committees which usurp Trade Union functions and responsibility and are contrary to the 1955 Congress decision:

In a state of society which is pledged to full employment, with a growing trade union organisation adding to its prestige and power in the community, there rests upon the Trade Union Movement a growing responsibility for a proper and adequate direction and control of its forces.

Because of the legal responsibilities that flow from legal registration of unions, under Commonwealth and State Industrial Statutes, together with added responsibility for unity and cohesion in industrial activities in their various forms, and the attainment of our political objectives to consummate our industrial and social aspirations, we recognise that development must proceed along the lines of greater Federal control of Trade Unions.

There must be a greater recognition by the trade unionist that he must accept direction and abide by properly constituted decisions by his union or executive.

Branches, sub-branches and District Committees of organisations, must have a greater recognition of their responsibility and consequences that flow both legally and morally from proceeding with actions in defiance of, or out of step with, the parent controlling authority, the Federal Council of their organisation, which is the legally recognised controlling body.

Accordingly, we draw the attention of future Federal Conferences of affiliated unions to this situation in the hope that they will discuss the implications involved and endeavour to strengthen effective direction and control of their membership and management.

We reaffirm the advantages of the A.C.T.U. conducting negotiations with Employers with a view to concluding industrial agreements in particular establishments or industries.

When such negotiations are concluded arrangements should be made by the Unions concerned in the negotiations for the resultant proposals to be brought to the notice of all members in the industries concerned and these members be then given the opportunity to declare themselves recognising in all cases the Federal Unions' authority to conclude these matters.

When a decision has been made it shall be binding on all concerned.

We are concerned that the actions of some area and shop committees and union officials have not assisted to smooth proceedings towards agreements, and we therefore urge upon all officials and shop committees the great advantages of their integrating their activities with those of the A.C.T.U. and the Unions concerned to the greater benefit of all concerned.

Therefore, the attention of the members of all Unions is drawn to Trade Union policy on these matters as determined by the 1961 Congress, particularly to the Charter which does not provide for Area Committees nor does it allow Shop Committees to deal with industrial matters affecting awards or Agreements, and we call upon them to use their influence to secure conformity with this policy.

The substantive content of the 1955 Congress decision, referred to above, is reproduced in identical language to comprise the five successive paragraphs of the 1963 A.C.T.U. Interstate Executive Resolution beginning 'In a state of society which is pledged to full employment', and ending 'effective direction and control of their membership and management'.

(c) *The Resolution of September 1964*

This Executive expresses its disapproval of the Unions acting contrary to the declared decisions of the Federal Organisations and Trade Union policy by coercing other unionists to participate in unauthorized industrial disputes. We remind all unions, officials and members, of the declared policy as determined by the ACTU Congress which defines the Charter of Shop Committees, and specifically precludes such Committees from usurping the functions of the Trade Unions in dealing with industrial matters covered by awards and agreements.

It is imperative for the proper functioning of Trade unionism that all sections of the Movement, officials and members alike, adhere to the policies and procedures determined by the Trade Union Movement.

That the acceptance by many workers of recent unnecessary and unauthorized actions by Shop Committees in calling mass meetings of workers in various establishments, indicates a complete lack of knowledge or appreciation by such workers of Trade Union policy and actions.

To correct this position, the Officers are authorised to provide to affiliated Unions and ACTU State Branches, the fullest information of such activities and policies for distribution to their members.

Attention is drawn to that part of the third resolution authorizing officers of the A.C.T.U. to furnish the affiliated unions, and the State Trades and Labour Councils, with the 'fullest information' concerning the policy and activities of the trade union movement in relation to shop committees, for purposes of dissemination among their members, so that these members would be in a position to understand the policy and become acquainted with the details of the activities of organized labour in this respect. It will be observed that a provision of this nature had found no place in the earlier resolutions of the A.C.T.U. dealing with the problem of shop committees and their kind; its introduction, and the education of the general body of workers in terms of it on an important industrial matter, could prove to be of significance in the efforts of the A.C.T.U. to protect recognized trade union authority against those who would assail it.

INDEXES

CASES

AWARDS

GENERAL

Federated Ship Painters' and Dockers' Union of Australia, 41,

Findlay, Commissioner, 89   [43-4

Fines, imposed on trade union, 82-4, 94-5, 112-13; imposed by trade union, 46-7, 49

Food Preservers' Union of Australia, 27, 63

Foreman, *see* Supervisors

Gallagher, Justice, 25-6

Gardner, Burleigh B. and Moore, David G., 52n., 58n.

Goodyear Tyre and Rubber Co. (Australia) Ltd, 90-2

Gough, Commissioner, 75, 82

Hammond, T. T., 2n.

Hartley, J., 3n.

Higgins, Justice, 58, 60

Hood, Commissioner, 23

Hughes, J. R., 4, 5

Industrial Arbitration Act, 1912-1963 (Western Australia), 12, 16n., 53, 65n., 118

Industrial Arbitration Act, 1940-1964 (New South Wales): section 25, 83; section 25A, 83; section 95, 65n.; section 99, 83; section 99A, 83; section 100, 82-4; section 111, 12; amendment in 1964, 82-4; *see also* Strike, illegal

Industrial Code, 1920-1963 (South Australia), 12, 65n.

Industrial Commission of New South Wales, 12, 18, 26, 53n., 54n., 69-70, 83; transcript of proceedings, 70n.

Industrial Conciliation and Arbitration Acts, 1961-1963 (Queensland), 12, 65n.

Industrial Court, South Australia, 12

Industrial Registrar, *see* Registrar

Industry, meaning, 99n.

Inherent power, doctrine, 46

Injunction (injunctive order), industrial, 76-7

Inspector of Labour, France, 65

Interstate Executive Resolution, A.C.T.U., *see* Australian Council of Trade Unions

Interview, *see* Right to interview

Isaacs, Chief Justice, 26n.; Justice, 42

Job delegate, 41; Report of Functions of Job Delegates on the Job, 38-40

Job Delegates Associations, 40

Job evaluation, 50

Job steward, 41

Joske, Justice, 63n.

Kelly, Chief Justice, 14n.

Killick, A. J., *see* Clegg, H. A., Adams, Rex and Killick, A. J.

Kirby, Justice, 75n.

Labour colleges, 21-2; *see also* Victorian Labor College

Latham, Chief Justice, 99n.

Leisure for workers, 20

Lenin, Nikolai, 1, 4

Lightning strike, 87

Lodge representative, 41

McMahon, William, 38, 113

Matthews, Commissioner, 29-30

Maynes, J. P., 3n.

Melbourne Trades Hall Council, 36, 71

Menzies, Sir Robert, 113

Metal Trades Employers' Association, 111n.

Miller, Delbert C. and Form, William H., 45n.

Milne-Bailey, W., 61n.

Minister for Labour and National Service, *see* McMahon, William

Minister of Labour, Great Britain, 55, 58n., 59n.

Ministry of Labour, Industrial Relations Handbook, Great Britain, 26n., 45n., 48n., 50n.

Morts Dock and Engineering Co. Pty Ltd, 31

National Joint Advisory Council, Great Britain, 55

Nevile, Justice, 52-5, 103, 117-19

N.J.A.C., *see* National Joint Advisory Council, Great Britain

Notification, *see* Conciliation and Arbitration Act 1904-1964, section 28

Office, meaning, 6, 11-14
Oil Refinery Employees (Shell Refining (Australia) Pty Ltd) Agreement, 92-3
O'Mara, Judge, 19, 65-6
Orders, under Conciliation and Arbitration Act 1904-1964: section 109, 75-7, 94-5, 111, 113-14; section 111, 113-14
Organizer, *see* Trade union
Origlass, N., 31-5
Overtime schedules, 50

Penal provisions, *see* Conciliation and Arbitration Act 1904-1964, sections 109 and 111
Penalty under Conciliation and Arbitration Act 1904-1964, *see* Fines
Peterson, Florence, 43n., 48n., 50n., 67
Piece-worker, and award, 69n.
Plumbers and Gasfitters Employees' Union of Australia, 64, 101
Political and Economic Planning study, *see* British Trade Unionism —Six Studies
Political canvassing, *see* Shop steward
Portus, Commissioner, 88-9
Practice, meaning, 67
Procedures, meaning, 107
Productivity, industrial, 85
Public policy, in relation to award-making, 67n.
Pulp and Paper Industry Agreement, 93

Ramset gun, 29-30
Rate fixing, 50
Registrar, Deputy Industrial, 28n., 114; Industrial, 28n., 60n., 83
Registration, *see* Cancellation of registration
Report of Functions of Job Delegates on the Job, *see* Job delegate
Report of the Committee on the Selection and Training of Supervisors, Great Britain, 58n., 59

Right of entry, 69-70
Right to interview, 28n., 67-70, 84-5
Roberts, B. C. (ed.), 2n., 38n., 50n.
Ross, W. D., 9
Roving delegate, 6n.

Safety, industrial, 29-30
St Mary's Project 590, 70
Seamen's Union of Australia, 6n., 41, 43n.
Secret ballot, *see* Trade union
Seear, Nancy, 38
Seniority rights, *see* Trade union
Settlement of disputes provision: in industrial award, 71-82, 90-2; in industrial agreement, 92-3
Sharkey, L. L., 2, 3
Shell Refining (Australia) Pty Ltd, 92-3
Shop area committee, *see* Committees, area and shop
Shop delegate, 41
Shop president, 41, 102
Shop representative, 41
Shop steward, 41; and safe working conditions, 29-30; political canvassing, 71; women, 62-3
'Shop stewards movement': in World War I, 24; in World War II, 24n.
'Sick' steward, 63-4
Spicer, Chief Justice, 94
Stalin, Josif, 2n., 4
Starke, Justice, 26n.
State Branches of A.C.T.U., *see* State Trades and Labour Councils
State Trades and Labour Councils, 57, 107-9, 115, 122-3, 125
Stevedoring Industry Act, 1956-1963, 25, 38n.
Steward, 41; *see also* Job steward, Shop steward
Strike, illegal, 83-4; unofficial, 24; *see also* Strike levies
Strike levies, 115
Supervisors: registration, 59-60; training, 58-9

Tariff Board, 10
Tasmania, regulation of labour relations, 13